It's Only Money!

A PRIMER FOR WOMEN

Allison Acken, Ph.D.

A WOMENTALKMONEY.COM BOOK

Design: Agostino Design, Woodland Hills

Published by:
womentalkmoney.com
PO Box 49327
Los Angeles, CA 90049
Orders@womentalkmoney.com

ISBN 0-9711715-1-3

Publisher's Cataloging-in-Publication
(Provided by Quality Books, Inc.)

Acken, Allison.
  It's only money: a primer for women / Allison Acken.
 — 1st ed.
  p. cm.
  Includes bibliographical references.
  ISBN 0-9711715-1-3

1. Women–Finance,Personal.   I. Title.

HG179.A35 2002   332.024'042
                QBI02-200217

Primer: "an elementary school-book for teaching children to read; by extension, a small introductory book on any subject; that which serves as a first means of instruction."*

Money: "current coin; metal stamped in pieces of portable form as a medium of exchange and measure of value. In modern use, commonly applied indifferently to coin and to such promissory documents representing coin (esp. government and bank notes) accepted as a medium of exchange."*

Opsimath: "one who begins to learn or study late in life."*

*Oxford English Dictionary, U.S. edition, 1985.

Dedicated to opsimaths everywhere

Contents

1. Our Favorite Phobia...1

2. Me and My Shadow..11

3. Ground Rules...23

4. Vive la Difference?..31

5. Fifty-Fifty Ain't Always Fair....................................43

6. Ladies First or I Was a Financial Moron..................53

7. Risky Business: Debt vs. Freedom..........................63

8. Row, Row, Row Your Boat Down The
    Income Streams...75

9. Some Day My Prince Will Come..............................89

10. A Pocketful of Miracles:
    Bag Ladies and Other Crises................................101

11. Crisis or Opportunity: Asking for Directions...........113

12. Don't Touch My God-forbid Money:
     A Lesson in Investment.........................127

13. We Can Do It, We Can Do It..............139

     Acknowledgments...............................151

     Appendix A...153

     Statistical References............................154

     Bibliography..157

It's Only Money!

A PRIMER FOR WOMEN

1. Our Favorite Phobia

Money may not buy happiness, but having enough money makes all the difference in the world. Charles Dickens said it best in *David Copperfield*: having a few pennies to spare after expenses, "result happiness" but being a few pennies short, "result misery." Notice that he was not talking about being wealthy, but just about having enough money to cover expenses, whatever they may be, and with a little bit left over. Today, too many women are living in Dickensian misery.

But then, there is that commonly-used little expression: "It's only money." We hear it often. Someone spends too much money, or loses a fortune, or makes a costly mistake, and we hear "It's only money." We'll say it ourselves if we go overboard. "It's only money." We say it with a wink or a laugh, or we may roll our eyes, but the irony is apparent.

Money is anything but "only" money when it comes to our

worries. Money is a vast unknown territory. Money can be scary. Money seems incomprehensible. Money feels unmanageable.

Even worse, money is paradoxical. Scary as it might be, money is appealing and useful to us. We want more of it. We like to have enough money around us. We know that money is necessary and critical to survival, but we have this belief that understanding money is beyond us somehow. What a combination!

Why is it so hard for us to deal with money? There are a million reasons for our ambivalence about money and we'll talk about all 1,000,000 of them later. *Really?* For now, I will say it again: "It's only money."

It's only money. It's only money. It's only money. Maybe if we say it again and again, like the lion in Oz, we'll be safe. Let's try it. "It's only money. It's only money. It's only money." Did it work?

If it's only money, why do we have so much trouble with it? Think about the other things we fear: spiders or bees, elevators or heights, darkness, dragons, thunder, the unknown. Rational or not to the rest of the world, our fears are based in some kind of reality: a bad experience, or a story we heard when we were children, or something we've been taught.

Being afraid of money isn't quite like those other fears because money is impossible to avoid. If we're afraid of the dark,

we can leave the lights on. If the fear is the elevator, take the stairs. If we're afraid of airplanes, we can drive to Brazil. However, no matter how hard we try, we cannot get away from money. Even a nun has to deal with money nowadays. Being afraid of money is like being afraid of the air we breathe. We can't do without it.

Metaphorically, women are stranded on Lake Money. We are sitting in the middle of the lake in a rowboat. Some of us have one oar; some no oars at all; some of us are in a boat with a slow leak; for some of us, the boat is sinking.

Not to scare you with too many statistics, here's the thumbnail. Even in 2002, women average somewhere between 70 to 74 cents in earnings compared to the men's dollar — a statistic that has barely changed in 25 years. During child-rearing years, much of our work is unpaid altogether. Most women will be working for most of their lives but in low-paid and less valued jobs — jobs with few benefits and very few pension dollars. Isn't that a pretty picture?

Even though we earn less, women pay more for goods and services than men do. Wait, get this: women earn 30% less than men but we pay more for goods and services. Shouldn't we be getting a 30% discount?

 $TATI$TIC:
Sixty-six percent of women's work is unpaid compared to 34% of men's work.[1]

This 30% disparity is a real shocker when you begin to tally it up. Think pantyhose. Think underwear, makeup, stockings vs. socks, purses vs. a wallet. Think haircuts, perms, coloring, or manicures, or cleaning bills. Think rowboat, one oar, slow leak, deep lake.

As if that isn't bad enough, let's look at the marketplace.

Advertisers torment us about looking fashionable. Our fashions change with each season and that ever-changing palette costs us dearly. Shades of white predominate one year; the next year, white is out. One season, you must wear long skirts; the next season, short skirts. Muted colors are in; muted colors are out. Wild patterns are a must; solid colors are a necessity. The changes are dramatic and costly. We don't have the equivalent of a navy blue blazer and gray slacks.

And here's the kicker: we live longer than men but with much less money put away for our old age. In other words, we get to be in worse financial shape from beginning to end. As the Church Lady used to say on *Saturday Night Live*, "Isn't that special?"

Feeling angry yet? Our more typical responses are worry and depression and shame. Let's take a look at the situation for a moment. Have we done this to ourselves? Do we deserve to be in this rotten rowboat? Of course, we do not. Then why do we put up with it? Think worry, depression, and shame: the three obstacles to money.

$TATI$TIC:

Almost half of working women earn less than $6.33 per hour.[2]

Most women who don't have enough money are worried sick about it — whether it's about paying the bills, coming up with the rent money, or taking care of the kids. We worry and worry and worry. Does it get us anywhere? NO! In fact, worrying is like running in place; we get worn out but without getting anywhere. Worrying uses up our energy. The only cure for worry is action.

Many women who don't have enough money are depressed

about it. We have internalized a bleak sense of our inability to do anything about money. We may have even heard these messages as children. Depression can be mean and debilitating and self-fulfilling. The cure for this brand of depression is to get a little angry — just enough to get moving forward.

WI$DOM:

"Money is not as mysterious or as powerful as we have been led to believe. Learn about it, get to know about it, begin to use it and not it you." - TYNE DALY

Too many women who don't have enough money are ashamed. We believe that something is terribly wrong with us, and that we've got to hide this big secret from the rest of the world or it will humiliate us beyond bearing. Shame is insidious and overwhelming. The cure for shame is to start talking about some of the secrets and the fears that are in our way.

Here's the #1 secret about money: it's only information. Furthermore, it's information that is pretty easy to learn. *WHAT?!!* No, truly, ninety per cent of us are smart enough to learn as much about money as we need to know. That's all we have to learn — only as much as we need to know — a little at a time. We don't have to learn one bit more than that.

Think of all the other information we've learned about cooking or sewing or relationships or cars or shopping or reading or writing or fashion or babies or makeup. It's all information, and we have learned a lot of it. Now the information we need to learn is about how to have enough money. So, let's roll up our sleeves, get a little angry, take some action, and start talking to each other about what we need to know.

Mind you, I do know that there are women who are terrific with money. They save and budget and invest. They own companies that are profitable, and they write books about money management. Those women had lots of good training at some point in their lives and managing money has become second nature to them, like boiling water or sewing on a button might be to the rest of us.

However, the rest of us have had little, if any, training about money. We certainly didn't learn about it in school. At home, we were taught about money just like we were taught our table manners. "Don't put your elbows on the table." "Do not talk about money." "Talking about money is impolite. It isn't ladylike." We were told that talking about money is tacky or *gauche* — depending on the neighborhood where we grew up.

As adults, when we look at the money-management books in the bookstore, we get anxious and overwhelmed. We become even more convinced that we'll never figure it out. We might even go spend some money to make us feel better. Those money-management books that are meant to be helpful are useless to us right now. We are, quite simply, not ready for them — yet. Right now, those books seem to us much like *War and Peace* would seem to a 5-year old.

"Yet" is an important little word. It means up to this moment, up to now. Here's a little psychological trick. If we can incorporate this one tiny word into our pronouncements about money, we will change our point of view. Honestly! "Yet" can change our P.O.V.

We might now say, "I just don't understand money." Let's add that one little word to the sentence. "I just don't understand money — <u>yet</u>." Hear the difference? The first statement has a dead-end kind of permanence to it. It reeks with the fatality of "and

I never will." But when we add this one powerful, little word, the implication is one of change: I don't understand money <u>yet</u>, but I will.

Slight changes in the way we say things can shift how we feel about any subject, including money. If we don't have any money saved <u>yet</u>, there is a sense that we will in the future. If we can't see how we're going to get out of debt <u>yet</u>, it implies that we will see our way out in the future. Try this one little change in the way you talk about money — it really works.

$TATI$TIC:

One of 7 women in America lives in poverty; 1 in 3 among African Americans and Latinas.[3]

Well, our secret is out in the open. We don't know enough about money — <u>yet</u>. We need to know more about money — making it, spending it, giving it away, holding on to it. So, what do we do now? It is actually fairly simple. We start learning. We do that by talking to each other about what we know and what we don't know. We're going to talk our way out of this mess.

In these pages, I will talk to you about what I've learned from other women and about my own experiences. I'll talk about some facts, share a few wise words about money from other women, and I'll suggest some resources for you. I'll ask you to try a few things that will move us toward more confidence with money.

We are in this predicament together and the best way for us to get out of it is to work together. We will desensitize each other to money so that we can have plenty of it around us without being afraid. We will say over and over again that we are going to have as much money as we need — and we'll get really clear about what that means for us as individuals. There is no one, absolutely right answer that will fit all of us, just like a size 10 doesn't fit every woman. From all of what we learn from each other, each of us will fashion a unique set of solutions that fits well.

The key is to work together, not alone. We will become our own Moneyworks, a women's factory, for making the building blocks to have enough money. We can do this a lot more easily if we work together. Ready?

Try this. Picture our Moneyworks in your mind. Not like those dingy factories of old, this 21st century Moneyworks is bright and cheerful with great music playing in the background, bread baking in the kitchen, and flexible work schedules. The women in the Moneyworks are working together to create the building blocks necessary for having enough money. In beautiful colors, there are earning blocks and saving blocks, getting out of debt blocks and investing blocks, taking a vacation blocks, and more.

Now, imagine yourself with all the building blocks you need to have enough money. In your mind, form a clear picture, a self-portrait, of you with more than enough money to pay the bills, to buy what you need, and to enjoy yourself. The "more than enough" part is really important; picture you with a little extra money left over. How does that feel? How big is that smile?

You may want to dance around the room in all those dollar bills. You may want to write a description or draw a picture of yourself with more than enough money around you. Hold on to that image because that picture is the goal. Just like the lion going to Oz, we are going to the land of having more than enough money.

Our Moneyworks is humming along. Can you hear it? "It's only money. It's only money. It's only money." *Hmmm.*

RESOURCES:

Your best friend will be your best resource in this learning process. You know you can talk to her about anything. If you can talk to her about your hips or your love life, you can talk to her about money.

2. Me and My Shadow

Seeing a portrait of ourselves with enough money is a delightful experience and it gives us an image of what our future can be. Now we have to back up and take a look at our current condition. It is a little like looking at our bodies in the mirror, and we know how much fun that can be.

One of the problems with money is that we can hide our money deficits. Most of us have been taught to not talk about money anyway, so it's particularly easy to hide what we don't know about money. In effect, we have been taught to hide.

That good ole' trio of worry and depression and shame leads us into self-blaming patterns that reinforce our hiding, and then we get into even bigger trouble with money. No wonder we feel like we're running around in circles. We are.

Other people can't see our money distress unless it's pretty extreme. It is quite possible to look great and to be in terrible shape financially. Just as it is possible to be in good shape financially, because of a high income or a trust or other source of support, but to know not the first thing about money. Either way, we are in far too vulnerable a position.

WI$DOM:
"Buy silver and hide it in the backyard."
— BLOSSOM DEARIE

When it comes to money, truly, looks can be deceiving. I know the worry-depression-shame complex only too well but you would never have suspected from looking at me. I am 5' 10" tall, with silver hair, a Ph. D. in clinical psychology, and a private practice on the West side of Los Angeles. The picture looks pretty good.

However, my own experience with money was extremely limited. I grew up in a single-parent family in the days when it was a rare occurrence. I won't go into the gory details about my father. Suffice it to say, that in the 50's and 60's when America was prospering at an astounding rate, my mother was left with two kids to support, my father's scandalous debts to repay, and no assets.

My mother did a good job of supporting my brother and me. We always had a roof over our heads and food on the table. She worked in a very successful record store and, because of that, we had experiences that most kids didn't. We met recording artists of the day like Perry Como, Robert Goulet and Billy Eckstine. Ever heard of these guys? In today's terms, it would be like meeting Sting or Tina Turner or Gwen Stefani or Garth Brooks. The occasional windfall would get us a trip to New York to go to the theater or a few days at the ocean.

We didn't learn about budgets, saving for a rainy day, investments, or owning property. Whatever money came in went right out again. In fact, my mother didn't have a checking account until she was 70 years old. During my childhood, all the bills were paid in person with cash or the occasional money order

I worked at a local theater in the summers and at the record store during the school year, and, like most teenage girls, I spent my money on clothes. The theater was really fun with a new production coming in every two weeks and a constantly changing cast of characters, literally. The theater was housed under a large circus tent with broad red and white stripes. I still remember those windy and wild thunderstorms when it took 10 of us to hold the tent down during a matinee. With opening nights and cast parties, I lived a rich and exciting life for a girl from Baltimore.

I honestly had no idea that my family was marginal economically. Everybody around us was in pretty much the same shape, except that all of my classmates lived in houses and we lived in a small apartment. They all had Dads and, somehow, I must have connected houses with Dads.

$TATI$TIC:

Forty percent of the nation's poor live in families headed by women.[4]

I didn't really get it until it was time to apply to college. That was a foreign concept in my family anyway; I was the first one to think about going to college. I hadn't worked hard enough to qualify for scholarships and there wasn't the money for me to go away to school. It was a real shock that I was going to be a commuter at the local state teachers' college. Of course, there were many kids from my neighborhood who didn't go to college at all, but most of my college-bound friends were going away to school.

Now, you might think that that would be the moment that I would have realized how important it is to have enough money, but it went right past me. In hindsight, I am amazed, but I just wasn't ready to get it then. It wasn't until much later, after my divorce and with responsibility for two children, when I began to understand how much I didn't know about money. Here's another secret about money: WHAT WE DON'T KNOW ABOUT MONEY WILL HURT US.

I started graduate school and got divorced at the same time. Big, big mistake! Actually, sometimes I think I've made every mistake in the money book. Not that I had much of a choice about the divorce. I had married very early and, except for two beautiful little girls, it was an unfortunate marriage.

Today, my psychotic optimism tells me that it all happened for a reason. I do know just how important it is for women to have enough money. (We'll talk about the concept of enough money later.) I understand a lot of what gets in the way for us, and I know a way out that is relatively painless. As I said before, we need to start talking about what we don't know about money and share with each other what we do know about money. It is that simple.

So, back to my story: I was the first mother on the block to get a divorce, with two little girls to support, and in my first year of graduate school. Although I did a couple of things right, the mistakes I made with the divorce settlement set us up for years of struggling that I could not see coming.

$TATI$TIC:

The standard of living for men who divorce goes up by 10%, while the divorced women's standard of living drops by 27%.[5]

The only financial asset in the marriage was the retirement fund from his job. I saw it as <u>his</u> money, and so did he. I couldn't afford a good lawyer; that compounded the situation. The bottom line was that I refused to ask for, much less fight for, my portion of this asset. My share would have put me through school and supported the girls — not to mention giving me future retirement benefits.

Next, I refused to take any alimony. Those were the days when feminism meant being a superwoman. I was a smart and strong woman fully capable of supporting myself, I thought. I had no idea what it would take to support two kids, or how meager child support judgments could be.

As if that weren't enough, I insisted on taking half of the debt because that seemed fair to me, 50-50. (Later, we'll talk about how 50-50 isn't always fair.) How stupid could I be? No alimony, none of the one asset, and half of the debt — what a deal-maker I was. And the lawyers and the judge all let me do this. It's shocking when I look back on it. If I had known only a little bit more — even a teeny bit — about money, I would have done things differently.

I don't think I talked to family or friends about much of this. Divorce was still an unusual and a shameful phenomenon. My brother was gone by this time, and no one else offered financial advice. I certainly didn't ask. I don't know if I would have taken advice if it had been offered. The worry-depression-shame complex is very powerful.

I must have looked like I was doing okay, but I was 27 years old and in a real mess. Most of my friends didn't have children, and they came from families with greater economic resources than I. I don't think they could even have imagined what my struggle was like.

$TATI$TIC:

Women represent 80 - 98% of workers in lower-paid jobs of librarians, bank tellers, nurses, child care workers, and typists.[6]

Aside from graduate school, the only other option I had, or could see, at the time was to return to teaching nursery school. I knew that wouldn't support all of us. At least in psychology, I had a chance at a much higher earning power. I decided to tough it out for a few years with the belief that, when I had finished school, we would be fine.

I applied for a tuition fellowship immediately and got it; that's one of the things I did right. I worked part-time, went to school full-time, and borrowed the rest of the money we needed. I had no understanding of what that would mean in the years to come. I got an excellent education, a Ph.D., *and a $50,000 debt to repay*.

At this point, my daughters were preteens, just moving into their most expensive phase. And I still had two years of low-paid internship work to do. What was I thinking? Truly, I wasn't thinking about it; I was just trying to get through it.

For the life of me, I could not understand why I could not get ahead. My classmates were buying new cars and houses, and travelling to exotic places, but the kids and I were stuck. I couldn't figure it out, but I was sure of one thing: there was something terribly wrong with me.

The day I realized that my rowboat was sinking fast was a day of true revelation. Thank goodness, I'll never forget it. I had purchased a computer set-up that was *only* going to cost $100 per month. I had made the decision in one of those "it's only money" moments but, a month later, I stared at the bill realizing with an intensely bright clarity that I simply didn't have another $100 on top of all my other monthly payments. I was stunned, frightened, and mainly ashamed — but I also knew that I needed to learn about money. I was like Scarlett O'Hara with that carrot.

I could tell you many painful stories about trying to hide my ignorance about money while I tried to figure it out, but I will tell you just this one at the moment. When my clinical supervisor was agonizing about buying an expensive desk for her new office, I said, "Oh, don't worry, it's tax deductible." She replied, "Yes, but I still have to come up with the money to pay for it." I didn't have the slightest idea what she meant — you may not either at this moment — but I tried to hide my embarrassment, and I laughed with her. All the while I was vaguely aware that she knew something that I didn't, and that it was probably something I needed to know. But how was I ever going to learn? I certainly wasn't going to ask her what she meant.

These feelings can be crippling. I could not bear to get near a book on money management, no matter how easy it purported to be. I was too scared and anxious. I wouldn't ask questions because I didn't want to look stupid. People always insist that there are no stupid questions, but I knew that mine would have been. Instead, I did stupid things like buying stuff that I couldn't afford so that we would look okay.

WI$DOM:

"Part of being a grownup — male or female - consists of learning about money. You can't turn it over to people who are smarter than you because the truth is that most of the people in the money business aren't smarter than you. I grew up understanding this in a serious and fundamental way, because the day my mother used her first Tampax, she bought Tampax stock: it turned out to be as good an investment as Xerox or IBM."   — NORA EPHRON

I finally got to the point that I could (covertly, of course) pick up a book about money in the bookstore as long as no one saw me. I am not kidding; my need to hide was that intense. As soon as I saw "budget" or "portfolio" or "compound interest" or some other term I didn't like or didn't understand, that book went right back on the shelf. I had a Ph.D., but I felt stupid and incompetent and overwhelmed — and wanted to hide even more.

I think it must be like not knowing how to read when you're an adult. Imagine what it would be like not to be able to read — a basic skill. Non-reading adults feel humiliated, and they work really hard to hide it from the rest of the world.

Knowing how to have enough money is as essential as knowing how to read. Not knowing enough about money can be just as shameful as not knowing how to read. Take it from an expert, hiding what we don't know only gets us into more trouble.

Slowly and over time, I began to be able to read a little bit about money. I started to notice articles in the paper, particularly articles about women and money. I actually started a file called "Newspaper Articles of Interest." Years later, I realized that all the articles in this file were about women and money. Unconsciously, that file was the beginning of this book, although I had no wild ideas about writing a book at the time, especially not a book about money.

One article about credit cards shocked me. It reported that, if you only pay the minimum payment due on a credit card, it takes over 20 years to pay off the balance — even if you never charged one more penny to that account. Suddenly and quite dramatically, I got it. I understood why I wasn't getting anywhere.

I was carrying a debt much larger than my yearly income, and it was growing like *The Blob*. I wasn't even keeping up with the interest. I was dutifully paying the minimum payment, then charging more. At that rate, I was never, ever going to be free of money problems. It was a total nightmare, and one that many American women are living right now.

If you are in debt, the most important thing about money you'll ever learn is to GET OUT OF DEBT AND STAY OUT OF DEBT. Notice the CAPS: that must mean it's really important. And, yes, it is possible to get out of debt although it may take a while.

(We'll talk more about debt later.)

So, that's my story. I made tons of mistakes before I started learning about money. I remember how intense my feelings of shame were, but now it's just a memory. I don't feel the pain anymore. I cannot begin to tell you what a relief it is to be rid of the shame. My financial life isn't perfect, and I certainly can still find something to worry about, but I don't carry that awful burden of secrecy. Money is information to me now. It's only money.

Try this. It's time to look at where you are with money right now. Think of yourself in a rowboat on Lake Money. Picture that rowboat you're sitting in. Does it have a leak or not? Is there one oar or two, or maybe none? How far from shore are you? Get as clear a picture as you can.

Look for one good sign: something that you are doing right with money. Find at least one piece of helpful information that you know about money. Do you remember how you learned it?

Start thinking about your background and experiences with money, and how you have come to where you are now. If you have a journal, you may want to start writing about your own history and process, but thinking about it is okay too.

`We're going to bail the water out of that rowboat if need be, plug up the leaks, find two oars, and build the muscles that we need to get our boats to solid ground. As we're rowing, remember that it's only money, it's only money, it's only money.

RESOURCES:

The newspapers and magazines in your home are good resources for small articles about money. Keep your eyes open for stories about women and money. You don't have to read a whole article if it makes you too anxious right now, but glance at some of the highlights.

3. Ground Rules

Because we are not used to talking about money, we have to create some ground rules. Without guidelines, we can be a little awkward or heavy-handed at first if we are not careful. The primary guideline is a simple "do unto others." We need to be respectful and gentle and kind — treat others the way we want to be treated.

Women are used to competing against each other — whether for a man, or top of the class, or other prizes. Often, we are not good sports with each other. We can be catty and gossip about other women. We can be so busy fighting with each other for short-term gains that we miss the more important goal of financial security or what I call having enough money.

Here's another secret about money: there is plenty of money to go around as long as nobody gets too greedy. Think about your best friend. Do you want her to have enough money? Of course you do. Does she want you to have enough money? Of course she does. Do you want to have enough money? Yes? Then, let's get to it.

$TATI$TIC:

Only 10% of working women make more than $12.67 an hour.[7]

Again, the first ground rule is to treat others as we want to be treated. The second ground rule is to listen with care. I mean that in both senses of the word. We must listen carefully to the content of our friends' words, and we must listen with caring and compassion. Some of the stories and thoughts we confide to each other will be painful and sad; obviously, they will require tenderness. Many of the stories we share will be funny because we do some really strange things with money. Keep in mind that, even when we are laughing, we need to take good care of each other.

Listening also means that we are paying attention to our friend's story, not thinking about what we want to say next. Really focus on what she is saying, what it means to her, and how she feels about it. We need to understand clearly if we are going to help each other.

The third ground rule is to be as honest about yourself as you can stand to be. That doesn't mean you have to force yourself to bare some deeply painful experience that you don't want to reveal. We are entitled to our privacy. For our purposes, honesty means that, whatever you decide to talk about, you will be as honest as you can.

When it's your turn to talk, pay attention to your own story and its details. What does it mean to you? How do you feel about it?

What would you like from your friend? How can she help you? She needs to understand you well if she is going to help you.

Fourth, be generous in sharing what you have learned. When you figure something out, tell your friend. If she already knows about it, that's great. Then you are both in good shape. If it's something new to her, you move forward together. Often, your newly learned piece of information will be something she's been desperately trying to figure out. In that case, you will have been a big help to her. That's the point: to help each other learn more about money.

The last ground rule is a big one: talk about *how*, not how much. This is a very important rule. If we're talking about how much, we are on the wrong path. How much is an absolute set-up for a win-lose game and, when it comes to feelings, win-lose games are not fun. We want to play a win-win game. We win; our friends win; other women and their families win. Nobody has to lose. There is plenty of money to go around. We need to focus on how to have enough money, not how much money somebody else has.

WI$DOM:

"Don't be shy about money. That's not the winner's way." – IVANA TRUMP

Have you ever been asked how much you make or how much you paid for something? There's no good answer to the question. If the number is too low or too high, you feel bad or they feel bad. It's just a downright embarrassing question. It's way too intrusive and, if we don't want to answer it, we look like we're being unfriendly when it's really the person who asked the question who is being rude, whether they know it or not.

I'll teach you a little trick for the times when someone asks you a "how much" question that you don't want to answer. Just smile and say, "If I tell you how much, I promise you that one of us will feel bad. If I got a better deal than you, you will feel bad and vice versa." In the long run, it will be better for you and for the person who asked the question.

$TATI$TIC:
Thirty-seven million wives work as cashiers, bank tellers, and temps to help their families get by.[8]

The "how much" can generate envy if you're talking about a lot of money, and envy feels terrible to both parties. A very dear friend of mine cannot stop himself from asking people how much they paid for their house. No matter what their answer, he ends up feeling bad. Either his house is worth less money than their house, or they made a better deal than he did, or theirs is bigger, or whatever. He has a good income, solid investments, and a very beautiful home, yet he keeps losing the "how much" game.

Talking about a small amount of money can be intimidating also. If we want to begin buying stocks, even if we have only a few dollars a month to invest, we can learn how to choose affordable and solid stocks. However, when we hear about large investors, we may feel like we don't belong in the stock market at all.

Every so often, the papers will report the death of a seemingly modest woman who left a small fortune to a school or some other cause. She had accumulated a vast amount of stocks, a little at a time. She would have been the woman that stockbrokers would have overlooked because she was a small investor. Who knows, they may have even intimidated her with stories of their rich clients.

The minute we start talking about how much, it is hard to avoid comparisons and competition. I have talked to a lot of women about money and I have never asked a question about how much money they have, or how much they paid for something, or how much money they earn in a year. That has made it easier for us to talk.

Obviously, if we want to buy something, we need to know the price; although there is that old, arrogant line that if you have to ask how much it costs, you can't afford it. When we are beginning to talk about money, the amounts can get in the way. If you have to make a choice between knowing how much and knowing how-to, go for the how-to.

So, unless you're looking at a price tag, stay away from questions about how much. We want to keep envy, intimidation, and competition to a minimum. We can talk about money without talking about how much. Aside from our curiosity, we don't need to know how much someone's house cost, or how much debt they had, or how much money they have in the bank. The important question is not how much, but how-to — that's what we really need to know.

<u>Review of the ground rules</u>:

- Be kind and respectful.
- Listen carefully and with caring.
- Be as honest about yourself as you can stand to be.
- Be generous in sharing what you have learned.
- Talk about how-to, not how much.

Our goal is to find out how other women learned to have enough money. How did she get out of debt? How did she start to save money? How did she buy her first house? How did she put herself or her kids through college? How did she increase her income? How did she decide which shares of stock to buy first? How did she deal with a crooked business manager? How did she take over the family business? How did she get off of welfare?

 **WI$DOM:**
"I believe women must take a more aggressive position in their understanding of the monetary affairs that affect their lives."
— RUBY DEE

And there are many more questions. How did she survive being single, divorced, widowed, or married, for that matter? How did she force her financial planner to explain things in a way she could understand? How did she start her own business? How did she recruit women for an investment club? Women just like us have done these things, even when they weren't sure that they could. We can too, once we have the information.

Are you ready? Remember that song? Here we go! No blame, no shame, no judgment, and lots of laughs as we crawl over this terrain together. We want to learn how to create new options for having enough money, and we want to enjoy ourselves along the way.

Now it's time to start talking to one of the women in your circle. It may be your best friend, your sister, a cousin, a neighbor, or a co-worker. Choose someone from a similar background and/or dealing with the same challenges as you are now — another woman who is in the same boat, so to speak. If you are a mother of young children, you might want to pick another mom who has little kids. If you are young and single, you may want to talk about money with another young, single woman. Most important, pick someone that you trust.

Explain to her that you are reading this crazy book about money that says all we have to do is start talking to each other. Give her the ground rules, and begin.

Try this. Pick one question or fear or secret about money that you've been carrying around for a while, and talk to her about it. If she's willing, let her tell you something about her issues with money. Once you do that, you're on your way.

Later, we'll get much more specific about issues; for right now, enjoy the process. Laugh, whisper and unburden yourself of that terrible secret or fear you've been carrying around. Let's end with a little chant: it's only money, it's only money, it's only money.

RESOURCES:

The internet can be a major resource, but many of the financial sites are way too complex for beginners. My Web site **(www.womentalkmoney.com)** is a simple place to get started.

4. Vive la Difference?

We can learn so much from other women. My friend J talked to me about the importance of role models.

J is a neuroscientist, world traveler, mother, wife, and great money manager. Professionally, she spends most of her time working with poor, drug-involved women and she has a strong message for us all, "There's nothing you can't do." She sees it every day in her work.

J learned that message early in her life from the women around her. Her ancestry is African American, Native American, and French-Irish folk from Oklahoma, Texas, and Louisiana. She grew up in an African American community where her mother was a schoolteacher, and the women in the neighborhood, Miss Ida and Miss Ella V., watched out for her.

In J's community, the women were a powerful support group for each other. As she puts it, "They had to be." In those days, the men were working on the trains, away for many days at a time. J had many positive role models around her and it shows.

Not that J didn't have some hard knocks: the day she arrived at UCLA for her first class in the doctoral program, the professor told her that the janitorial staff was not allowed to sit in on classes. Another young woman might have crumbled in the face of this, but not J. She took the hurt and summoned up her ancestry, the women who had raised her, and her own pride to tell this jerk that her degree was from one of the best schools in the country, and that she was a *bona fide* student in "his" doctoral program.

Most of us didn't have the kind of positive modeling that J had, but we did have role models. That's part of what we need to sort out. The term "role models" has been overused, but the concept of modeling is incredibly important.

What are our models of women and money? We have society's picture of the ideal woman. We have individual models mainly from our families and a few teachers. And we have the images of incredibly successful women who are held up to us as role models.

$TATI$TIC:

The number of married women working outside the home has nearly tripled since 1951.[9]

Society's picture is a bit confusing. The ideal woman of today is supposed to get an education, have a career, and be able to support herself. She is still expected to marry, have children, and be a good wife and mother. If finances permit, she is a stay-at-home mom and, if not, she will work outside the home, but the primary goal is that she be a good wife and mother. We have a fuzzy picture of her life after that. She may return to the workplace when her children are in school or grown, and she is to age with a quiet grace, and become a wonderful grand-mother. Or something like that.

WI$DOM:

"Save for a rainy day." — DINA MERRILL

Here's the real picture for the majority of American women. You remember that income gap? That's just the beginning. A very small percentage of single women are property owners. Most women who do own property are co-owners with their husbands and, in States with separate property laws, whoever earns the most money is the legal owner of the property. Gee, that's fair! I wonder who wrote those laws?

Most married women with children are working outside the home. The number of women in poverty, particularly women with children, is very high. Divorce is frequent. Many widows are ill prepared financially for the death of their husbands. Women of retirement age, even if they have pensions, are living on very modest incomes. And, sadly enough, many women of all ages are hoping for a Prince Charming to rescue them. (Poor Prince Charming!)

Today, many elderly women are trying to manage on very small incomes. "Baby Boomer" women are beginning to see that, unless they do something soon to prepare for their older years, they will be living at the poverty level. Young women who look at the financial condition of their mothers and grandmothers are worrying about their future. No wonder we get depressed.

There are some bits of good news. Women have learned how to earn money and how to support themselves and others. We are working hard. Beyond that, we are not taking care of ourselves, much less planning for our future. If this sounds familiar, you are not alone. That's the reality for most women.

Now, let's talk about our individual role models. There are four kinds of models that affect us. By the way, we fit into one of these categories too. Like it or not, we are models for others: the little girl you baby sit, your niece, your own child, your sister, cousin, aunt, mother, and grandmother.

Modeling doesn't just go from older to younger, although we do tend to think of it that way. No matter how old we are, we can be, and probably are, models for other women in our lives. As we begin to learn more about money, we may very well help teach our grandmothers or mothers about money too.

Let's talk about the easiest and best kind of modeling first. We'll save the worst for last. Our positive-positive models are the women who have our best interests at heart and who know a lot about money. You probably didn't have this kind of model or you wouldn't be reading this book; you would be more like my friend J.

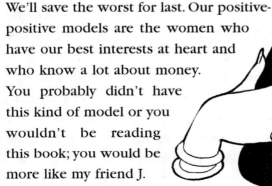

Our positive-negative models are the women who may care about us and treat us well but who are terrible with money. Most families have the lovable relative, maybe an Aunt Jane, who would give us the world — if only she had it. They are good models when it comes to caring about us, but when it comes to finances, they can't seem to hold onto two nickels. They'd love to help us, but they can't.

Then there are the negative types: women who treat us miserably but clearly know a lot about money, and the women who treat us poorly and don't have good money skills. In my book, the woman who has the skills but won't help is the worst kind of model: the Queen Bee who needs to keep everything for herself. She doesn't wish you well, or want to help you, or want you to get ahead. If you have a mother or grandmother like that, you have felt their sting. Money issues may be even tougher for you than you know.

Positive models, the women we want to be like, are the models we all wish we had. These positive models are doing well, and they teach us in a kind and gentle way, increasing our chances both of learning and of being able to retain the information for our own use.

We've all had at least one really good teacher in school, someone who was smart and kind and tough when need be, who knew the information, and who enjoyed helping us understand the material even if they had to go over it many times. No matter how long ago, we still remember how that teacher's attitude affected us. For you, it may not have been a teacher but your grandmother or your first boss — someone who wanted you to succeed at the task and was willing to devote time and energy to help you. It's this person we need to keep in mind when we are talking to each other about money.

The person we don't want to be like is the negative role model. An extreme example would be a person who gambles away the paycheck regularly or the woman who spends the rent money on a pair of shoes. An equally extreme example on the other end of the spectrum is the person who is so frugal that money is never spent on anything, particularly fun — Ebeneezer Scrooge comes to mind. We don't want to be like either of these models.

Here's where it gets less clear. Some of us grew up with parents who were good people in many ways, loving and kind providers, but who were lacking in the ways they dealt with money. We may have learned many valuable skills from them, but we may have also picked up unsound information about dealing with money — information that is getting in our way today. Even more common was to have good parents who, nevertheless, gave off negative messages about our ability to handle money: that money is above us or beneath us in some way.

Some parents are too impatient to teach. Some do things for their children either because they want to keep control over their children or because it's easier for them, even if it isn't good for the children. These parents seem to not realize that their job is to help their children develop the skills to do it for themselves.

In addition to these negative role models, there are people who have authority but who treat us negatively. Too many of us have had a bad teacher, an insensitive boss, or a mean coach who has had a negative effect on us. Even worse is having a father or mother who gave consistently negative and destructive messages like "fat, stupid, ugly, you'll never understand money." Those words from parents are terribly damaging because parents have so much power with their kids. Kids believe what their parents tell them.

Now, let's look at the superstars whom we are told are our role models, women like Oprah or Julia Roberts or Barbara Walters or Toni Morrison or the supermodels. Here's my question about these superstar role models: Can anyone be Oprah? Here's my answer: I don't think so.

Superstars are extraordinary women with extraordinary accomplishments. They are extremely gifted, talented, hard-working women who have had great good fortune. They are so far removed from the rest of us that we have no idea what their lives are really like. We tend to idealize their lives, but they have struggles of their own — sometimes even with money.

We are stunned when Julia Roberts has another failed relationship. At the Oscar Ceremony in 2001, she announced her undying love for Ben Bratt to the whole world. Just a few weeks later, her face was plastered all over the tabloids when he broke up with her.

Judy Collins, a mega-successful singer-songwriter, woke up one day to find that her money managers had misappropriated her earnings. Instead of being wealthy, she owed the IRS a small fortune. She appeared at a women's conference in the 1990's to talk about her story. Her message for all the women waiting for a Prince Charming: "NO ONE IS COMING!"

When I began to work on this book, I wrote to a number of celebrity women to ask for their advice about money. About 30 of these women were generous enough to respond with their WI$DOM. I had written to celebrities of all ages but the preponderance of responses was from women over 50. Trisha Yearwood was the only young woman who wrote back.

WI$DOM:

"As a banker's daughter, I'd have to say never let anyone else "take care" of your money for you. My father taught me to balance   my first checkbook in high school. Know your own business and take responsibility for where your money is invested and how it is spent."   — TRISHA YEARWOOD

A number of the comments from these celebrities are about saving, pensions, and retirement. All of these women are great successes in our eyes. We would imagine them to have all the money they need, yet their advice is to save, save, save. Do you think they're trying to tell us something?

The most startling comment came from a woman who is recognized the world over. She has been a phenomenally successful television star. No, I won't say who she is. She wrote back, "I'm not being facetious, but I don't know anything about money." Her real life is completely different from the roles she has played. Extraordinary women are in touch with their money to a greater or lesser degree just like the rest of us.

Don't get me wrong. I am not saying that you aren't an extraordinary woman. You may be. If you have a special talent or gift or are extraordinarily beautiful and you are willing to work very hard, I will only encourage you. It will take some good fortune and good choices to get you to the top, but go for it. Use your own positive models to learn what you need to know.

Ask for help when you need it, and take the advice of the women in these pages.

In some sense, we are all extraordinary women, and we all need to be much more capable with money. Unlike the persistent myth of the traditional family, most of us will be working outside the home during our adult lives. We will earn money as single women, wives/partners, second-income mothers, single parents, middle-aged women, widows, and older women. Many of us will be responsible for supporting not just ourselves but our children, elderly parents, or disabled partners.

We need more portraits of success. We need to *be* portraits of success. Women of all ages need positive, female models. This is particularly true for younger women who can expect to be in the workplace for most of their adult lives. Very few younger women had models to accurately reflect the 21st century woman.

One 22-year old daughter told her father that she is much more comfortable talking with him about money because her mother scares her. This concerned father asked his daughter if she worries about money. She replied that she doesn't worry because she knows he will always be there to help her. Many young women with good fathers cannot even conceive of the time when their fathers will not be there — and their fathers don't want to think about it either. Like a lot of us, it will hit her later that she won't always have her father to count on.

Today's young women, if they were raised in traditional families, saw an at-home mother who may have been very active in community affairs but not in the workforce. These young women cannot look to their fathers as their models, terrific though they might be as fathers, because the issues are different for men and women. Remember that lovely 30% disparity? (Later on, we'll talk about glass ceilings.) I am not saying that a father cannot teach his daughter about money; of course, he can. What he cannot do is model a 21st century *woman* for his daughter.

Many young women have grown up with mothers who worked outside the home, but who have had trouble balancing those roles. Very successful women have been forced to make tough choices because of the demands of their careers and, believe it or not, many of them do not teach their daughters about money. Young women raised in the working class, or in the single-parent families that have proliferated since the 1960's, have seen mothers overloaded by their dual roles, and who still don't have enough money. They are not models for these young women to emulate, and their mothers wouldn't wish it on them either.

$TATI$TIC:

Women are 40% of the workforce, but only 5% of senior executives are female."

Girls and young women need more role models. *We* need more role models. We need to *be* role models, for them and for each other. Women need to know that, just like driving a car or using a hammer, or talking about sex, learning about money can make us feel more confident and in-charge. Money won't make us happy, but it sure can make life easier. What can come with money is a sense of power, both at home and in the workplace.

Talking about money and how it works is a step toward having more power in our lives and it may seem like a big step at first. As the old joke says, "That first step is a lulu." We may have as much trouble talking about money as we did talking about orgasms in the olden days, but it'll be worth it.

Our modeling, both positive and negative, is the perfect topic to delve deeper into our money history. You've picked the friend that you feel comfortable talking to about money. You've got the ground rules down, and you've talked about at least one fear or secret. (If you haven't and don't feel ready to start talking yet, try to keep a journal and go solo for the moment.)

Try this. Let's get specific and talk about the negative models first. You might want to burn some sage and clear the air of these negative notions. Get them out in the open, and then get rid of them. They've been getting in the way for too long.

Then, talk about the positive models and the good feelings internalized because of them. You may want to push back the curtains and open the windows. Think about what they taught you about money and your abilities with money. What do you wish they had taught you? What is the most important thing you want to know about money?

Repeat our mantra: it's only money, it's only money, it's only money.

RESOURCES:

If you want a terrific book to read, pick up Bebe Moore Campbell's "What You Owe Me." She handles issues of money, diversity, and the family process in a powerful and eminently readable way.

5. Fifty-Fifty Ain't Always Fair

Ever agree to have lunch with a guy and find yourself in an expensive restaurant of his choice? You think he will pick up the check but, just in case, you order very carefully from the right side of the menu. You watch him eat three courses while you munch slowly on your lettuce leaves. Then, with a flourish, he orders the restaurant's specialty, a chocolate *soufflé*, to be followed by espresso. When the check arrives, he says, "Let's just split it." That is 50-50, but is it equal? Not in my book, it's not. So, how did we get here?

The economics of relationships shifted in the 20th century, some for better, some for worse. Before that, very few women worked outside the home to generate income. Women were dependent financially on their fathers, husbands, and brothers. An even cursory reading of Jane Austen, Charlotte Bronte, Louisa May Alcott, and George Eliot underlines the difficulties of this dependency. Of course, there were the spinsters who were teachers or nurses or household workers, and a few scholars, scientists, and physicians, but, by and large, women's work was in the home.

$TATI$TIC:

In the late 19th century, only 13% of American women worked outside the home.[12]

In the very olden days of rural life, survival depended on everyone's labor. Food preparation was as important as working in the fields — at least that's how it looks to us now. As the urban, industrialized environments developed, the men went out to work for MONEY and women kept the home. That was equal.

At some point, money became an end in itself: the more money, the more status. And guess what happened? Men's work = money = power. Women's work = no money = no power.

The rhetoric still hailed Mom and apple pie as top values, but society's focus was the money.

The war effort of the 1940's pushed women into the work force to replace the men who went overseas. Not only were women covering the desks and offices, but they were also building airplanes and "manning" the factories. California and other states developed a massive system of state-supported childcare to make this war effort possible — stunning when you look at how difficult it is for parents to find affordable child care today. Women kept the country running while the men fought at the front. Women were earning money in significant numbers for the first time.

WI$DOM:

"Keep your money. Fall in love. But keep your money." – LINDA ELLERBEE

After the war was over, the men who returned went back to their jobs, and the women went back into the homes. The suburban life of the 1950's was invented, and advertisers coaxed women back into their aprons to enjoy the modern conveniences of homemaking. Donning their cocktail hats in the evenings, the housewives greeted their husbands as they returned home after a hard day at the office.

Even one episode of *I Love Lucy* will tell you most of what you need to know about the 50's. Why do you think Lucy and Ethel came up with all those hair-brained, moneymaking schemes? And how many times does Lucy try to hide her new hat from Ricky? She's always got "some 'splaining to do."

Two major effects of WWII were the booming economy, the likes of which we may never see again, and the huge number of babies born. The daughters of those Post-WWII women are today's Boomers. The first of those daughters reached high school with many more opportunities for advanced learning and career choices than their mothers had.

$TATI$TIC:

In 1940, 1 of 4 workers was female. 1 of 8 women worked as domestics. By 1950, only 1 of 15 worked as domestics; by 1995, only 1 of 100.[13]

The later Boomer girls could choose among opportunities in law, medicine, science, and engineering — unprecedented choices. Though not necessarily equal, possibilities existed as never before. It was a time of incredible change and hope and, ultimately, disappointment.

The 60's and 70's saw political upheaval that would not have been imagined by earlier generations. The country went from Camelot to chaos. This period saw almost unbelievable tumult including: the ugly battles over integration of schools; the murder of a president; growing opposition to a faraway war; the assassination of four major leaders; riots in the streets; a man on the moon; the decision of a president not to seek a second term; political scandal in the White House; the return of soldiers in defeat and derision; the resignation of a disgraced president; and, the renewal of the Women's Movement.

In a brief 15-year period, traditional American society was changed forever. We witnessed the death of heroes, both literally and figuratively. Soldiers no longer revered, heroic leaders assassinated, the presidency in shambles — America was left without its male icons and with a loss of respect for authority in general. Women were struggling to find some sense of equality. There was an intense focus on the individual, ergo the "Me" generation, resulting in a huge increase in divorce rates.

The 80's and 90's saw technological advances that even science fiction films didn't predict. Have you ever noticed how few women are in those films? The computer, a mammoth in the 50's, had been reduced to human proportions and became a personal necessity by the end of the century. Women entered the workforce in vast numbers, and they were represented in many more non-traditional job categories than in previous decades.

Forgive this truncated historical litany, but it is important that we understand how we got to where we are now. Rosie the Riveter became Lucy Ricardo. Their daughers became the "Me generation". Their daughters are the techno-savvy young working women and young mothers of the 21st century.

So, is it all better now? Did all of that turmoil in the last few decades of the 20th century put women on an equal footing economically? Truly, with a few exceptions, the answer is no. Does it sound too crazy to say that I think we're getting there?

$TATI$TIC:

In 1970, 40% of women were in the workforce. By 1991, the figure grew to 69%.[14]

Money is the next important personal agenda for American women. We now have access to education and job opportunities as never before. Younger couples are working very hard to establish equal partnerships in their personal relationships. (We'll talk about relationships later.)

Many families today are two-income families by necessity but, oops, there's still that 30% disparity in income. The imbalance in division of household chores has found its way into the 21st century also. Remember the old adage: Man works from sun to sun, but women's work is never done. How equal is that?

Not to deny the positive changes that have occurred, we still need more. Equal needs to be equal — really equal, not just 50-50. There's this weird psychological phenomenon wherein women, unlike men, tend to blame themselves for their problems and to overly attribute their successes to luck. We're really amazing when you think about it. If something is wrong, like if we are paid only 70 cents on the dollar for our work, it must be our fault.

The *status quo* continues on, or it has so far. A gain of 5 cents in 30 years is pretty static. We need to recognize that this disparity is not an individual problem. It's a problem for all women, and it should be a problem for the people who care about us.

As if that weren't enough, the long-standing American dream tells us that everyone has an equal chance, and that any child can grow up to be President or a self-made man. Is it the American dream or the American fantasy? Whichever, this widely-held belief is problematic.

The first problem is both obvious and subtle at the same time. Equal is a concept that has troubled America historically. The long battle over "separate but equal" education is the best example. What is equal? Remember that 30% disparity? If women make 30% less, but split expenses 50 - 50 with men, I think it's a real stretch to call that equal. Money is not a level playing field.

The second problem is that we haven't had a female President — <u>yet</u> — and probably won't for many years. As for self-made women, there are many successful women but most of us don't have ready access to them. The wildly successful women of the entertainment business seem so far away from most women's experiences, in part because we only see the results of their success. We seldom are privy to the process by which these women made it. Most of these women have worked long and hard to achieve what we often think of as overnight success.

Then there's the problem of class. We all have it, but does it work for us or against us? If we're all equal, our socioeconomic origins shouldn't have any effect on our economic future. Right? Although much more is being written about SES in the USA in recent times, it remains a hot topic that makes people really uncomfortable. America is not supposed to have a class system; that's for England or India.

The truth is that it is only human to need some means to differentiate and categorize. We need to know that green means go and red means stop, or that a growling dog or a charging bear means danger — not that we run into too many charging bears nowadays. But somewhere along the way, the process of differentiating, meaning how things are different, turned into discrimination with a value judgment attached, meaning how things are good or bad, better or worse.

Discrimination goes back a very long time. There is a story my old statistics professor told about Aristotle determining that women were inferior because they had fewer teeth than men. In fact, women and men have the same number of teeth. As that professor said, "Wouldn't you think he would have at least counted?"

Most discrimination is based on feelings, not on data. Data tell us facts: there are more apples than oranges in the fridge, or that family has more money than this family, or the average man is taller than the average woman. When feelings and judgments get into the mix, we draw conclusions that taller is better, or apples are better, or that the family with more money is better than the family with less money. That's discrimination.

When it comes to socioeconomic backgrounds, our challenge is to look at the data and recognize differences without making judgments. In some households, there is simply very little money to manage; they are almost always in the hole or catching up. They are worrying about how to pay for the cornflakes, while other households are following the top 10 yields in the *Wall Street Journal*. Of course, most people are somewhere in the middle, struggling to make ends meet. The rising costs of medical care and education are stretching most of these families' resources to the breaking point. A little compassion for each other will go a long way.

We already know about the disparity of gender. Now, if we are willing to consider that our class affects our economic well-being, we then add the effects of ethnicity. Who has the highest probability of success: the daughter of a single mother on welfare, two working parents, or a wealthy family? Does family ethnicity change the chances for success?

Some women are playing triple jeopardy, and it's a hard game to win. However, it really helps to know what game we're playing. It's one challenge if the game is double jeopardy, quite another if the game is triple jeopardy.

Let's have a little compassion for ourselves. We need to know where we are starting, so that we can mark our own progress realistically. We must be our own reference point. Let's compare us to us, not to somebody else.

A young woman who finishes college with $30,000 in school loans to pay back will feel discouraged if she compares herself to someone whose education costs were paid by her family and who received $10,000 in cash, plus a new car, as a graduation present. If we have a realistic picture of where we start with money, we will feel better about our own growth and development.

$TATI$TIC:

In the 1950's, only 2% of MBA graduates were women; in 1998, women take 37% of the MBA's. [15]

The same thing is true about what we know or don't know — <u>yet</u> — about money. Try to maintain a developmental perspective. Some women have learned more information about money than others have learned <u>yet</u>. Some may have gotten off to a good start with their mother and/or father teaching them a lot about money. Others may have not started to learn until a divorce, single parenthood, death, or other event shifted their lives forever.

Here's another tip: watch out for stereotypes. Some women who grew up in wealthy families learned more about money and learned earlier than women who grew up in poor households, but sometimes just the opposite is true. Rich women may have more money than other women do, but they don't necessarily have more know-how. Knowledge about money is the critical element.

Knowledge about money is what we're going for. Then maybe we can knock that 30% disparity on its ear. Shall we? Remember that other old saying that if we don't learn from history, we are doomed to repeat it.

Time for a breather. There's a lot of information to digest. Let's get up and stretch and take in some fresh air — a fifth chapter stretch. How about being just a little silly? For some reason, this chapter kept bringing song titles into my head. Maybe it's thinking about different eras that did it, maybe just needing a little comic relief.

There are so many songs about money: "Money" by Pink Floyd; the Beatles recording of "Money, That's What I Want"; "Half a Sixpence"; "Ten Cents a Dance"; "The Money Song" from Cabaret; "I Found a Million-dollar Baby (in a 5 & 10-cent Store)". Remember the lyric from Neil Diamond's "Forever in Blue Jeans"?

I told you it was pretty silly. Are any lyrics popping into your head? Make a list, invent a matching game, or just sing out loud. Maybe we'll write a song called, "It's only money, it's only money, it's only money."

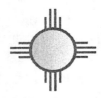

RESOURCES:
The older women you know have stories to tell about their eras. You might want to ask your grandmother, great-grandmother, mother, great aunt, or other older woman in your circle about her sense of women and money when she was your age.

6. Ladies First, or
I Was A Financial Moron

adylike is a term that we don't hear very often nowadays, but it is a concept that many of us heard growing up. Certain ways of behaving, speaking, moving, sitting and thinking were deemed to be ladylike. The dictionary's definition is "well-bred, polite, refined." When we were told to not talk about money, it was often under the guise that it wasn't ladylike.

It reminds me of a children's story called "Ladies First." If you were a little girl or a young mother in the 1970's, you may remember a record called *Free to Be You and Me.* Organized by Marlo Thomas, a group of actors and singers created this collection of stories and songs. In recent years it has been re-released on CD, and I heard a young mother playing it for her two little girls a few weeks ago.

"Ladies First" is about a little girl who always wants to be first.

In an obnoxious little voice, she is constantly saying, "Ladies first, ladies first." The climax of the story comes when she and other children are confronted by a lion; she pushes her way to the front saying, "Ladies first, ladies first." The punch line is that the lion eats her first. So much for being a lady!

$TATI$TIC:

The numbers of single mothers increased by 33% from 1980 (5.8 million) to 1990 (7.7 million).[16]

When I spoke to writer Carolyn See about money, she talked about her struggle to be ladylike. If you don't know Carolyn's work already, you're in for a treat. Her memoir, *DREAMING: Hard Luck and Good Times in America,* and her most recent novel, *Handyman,* were both on the *NY Times* best-seller list. As part of a trio that included John Espey, the consummate gentleman with whom she lived for many years, and her daughter Lisa, Carolyn wrote romance novels under the *nom de plume* of Monica Highland; these books sold several million copies. Today, Carolyn is a professor at UCLA and a great help to other writers.

Carolyn has a fresh, saucy, irreverent, charming and wise take on money and relationships between men and women. She grew up in a wild household with a charming, ne'er do well father and a crazy, literally, mother who threw her out of the house when she was 16 years old. Carolyn managed to get herself through high school, college, marriage and children, and into a Ph.D. program. Then divorce turned her life upside down.

Carolyn describes herself as a "financial moron" at that point in her life. The concept of ladylike was very important to her, but she didn't quite know what it meant. She made up a definition: "not smoking, not learning to drive (in Los Angeles), and not writing a check." She handed over all of her income to her husband which "he then spent on OTHER WOMEN." She was facing divorce, and disabled by being ladylike.

When she talks about having to write a check for the first time, it makes you want to laugh and cry at the same time. She was petrified, shaking all over, and "sweating bullets" trying to fill in the spaces on that first check. Carolyn went through many hard times raising her daughters and making a living; she has a great recipe for feeding four on $5 "including wine." Her story moved on to much happier ground with great success and wonderful relationships. She left those notions of being ladylike behind her.

Not all stories turn out so well. I remember a perfectly horrid moment when I was 21 and about to be married. Sitting in the well-appointed living room of my future mother-in-law's home, we chatted about the scheduling for a wedding-related event. My mother's work schedule was interfering with my mother-in-law's plans. This woman looked me straight in the eye, saying that she really liked my mother because she was so much fun. I didn't see it coming, but then she said, "Of course, a real lady never works."

$TATI$TIC:

The average working woman's family would earn $4,205 more per year if women were paid as much as men with comparable job qualifications.[7]

The next few moments are still blurry; I don't even know if I said anything to her. From the complex of feelings — shock, protectiveness, anger, shame, and guilt — I realized how much this "lady" did not like me, or my family's circumstances. All of this was communicated through her judgment that my mother was not ladylike.

In that women's world, being ladylike meant not generating income and not handling money. I thought of the women who worked in the record store with my mother: Betty Seidel, Mary Massimini, Dot Briel. Were they not ladies? If they weren't ladylike, was I? More important, was ladylike something I wanted to be? So much power was contained in that one word.

While many women of her generation (the post-World War II moms) did not work outside the home, they were heavily involved in child-related and charitable work in the PTA, Scouts, their churches and temples, and their favorite causes.

My then mother-in-law did not drive and she neither worked in a job nor had any of these charitable activities; but she was, in her estimation, a lady. She was dependent on her husband until his death, and then on her mother. After her mother died, she was dependent on her brother who managed her money. Sadly, he made some very poor decisions and lost most of her funds. She died in a board and care situation. In my mind, it was a huge price to pay for being a lady.

WI$DOM:

"Whether riding a horse, piloting an aircraft or charting your financial future, you have to stay on course. It's imperative to clearly define your goals and have the determination to see them through, keeping in mind that it may be a bumpy ride now and then. Stay motivated and the end result will be the realization of your dreams." — ROBYN ASTAIRE

Let's talk about dealing with money. Contrary to some, I believe that making money, having money, managing money, and investing are very feminine activities. Women have been notorious as consumers; we love buying beautiful things and shopping at sales. We are very careful to assess the values of our

clothes, the foods we choose at the market, and the appliances we buy for our homes. In the same way we decide which outfit or which model of toaster to buy, we can choose an investment — be it a house, a savings vehicle, or stocks. Having enough money can be very sexy, so what gets in our way?

Part of the problem is that we've gone plastic. Money used to have an obvious reality to it. We made only so much and had only so much to spend; then it was gone. Credit cards have distorted this picture beyond recognition. (We'll talk more about credit cards later.) Suffice it to say that our reality about money has gotten really fuzzy, and that can distort our decisions about spending.

Ever say the words "I deserve it" when faced with a desirable item? Those three little words can get us into big trouble. We've all run up against this: a new car, a designer dress, another pair of shoes, or an out-of-sight purse that we would really love to have.

With all the talk today about self-esteem and taking care of our selves, it can get really confusing. Whether or not we "deserve" to have that designer dress or, on a larger scale, to live in an expensive home is not the correct question. Whether or not we have the money to afford it is the question, but we hate to hear that question.

Let's look at two possibilities. One woman earns $200,000 a year and has no debt, but she does not feel she "deserves" to have a $500 dress. This woman probably needs to focus on her self-esteem and the internal conflicts that contribute to her feeling that she doesn't deserve it. However, the picture is very different for a woman who earns $20,000 a year, has $12,000 in credit card debt, and wants to buy the $500 dress because she "deserves it" even if she "can't afford it." She is a good, hard-working woman. Of course she deserves to have that dress, but is it a good idea for her to buy it?

What do we say if she asks us if she should buy it? If we want to be a good friend, what will we say? We'd probably all agree that the first woman needs support to buy the dress — that one's pretty easy. Saying yes is usually much easier than saying no.

$TATI$TIC:

The average credit card debt for college students is $1,843; 5% have more than $7,000 in credit card debt.[18]

It's the second scenario that is much harder for most of us. She really wants the dress, she looks great in it, and she has a hot date this weekend. Sound familiar? She doesn't have the money, so she would have to charge it; but we knew that would be the case. We all want to say, "Go for it." And we might, but, next time this happens, think about what it might really mean for her.

This one dress is worth about two-weeks' pay, or a month's rent, or six weeks worth of grocery money. Still want to say yes to her? If she charges it and pays it off over time, it will cost her another $75 a year or so. What do we say now? Is it a good idea for her to buy this dress?

If we've had a similar experience, it will color our answer. If we bought the dress, had a great time on the date, and got a big raise the next week, we might think it's a great idea for her to buy the dress. If we bought the dress, but the date was a bust, the dress got stained beyond repair, and we had to look at that bill for months, we will have a different opinion.

Our experiences, our fantasies, and our information base all color how we look at money. The messages we have internalized are very powerful. The new information base that we are building will mediate some of those internal, "I deserve it" messages.

"Rescue me." We might never say these words out loud but the fantasies abound. And for good reason: we learned them. I hear them frequently from women who are wishing for someone to save them, carry them off, or whatever the fantasy might be.

Keep in mind that these fantasies don't come from nowhere. We teach them to young girls still. Just take a look at the media if you doubt it.

In the classic Disney movies, *Sleeping Beauty* and *Snow White* are both waiting to be rescued. Sleeping Beauty is, literally unconscious about it. However, Snow White sings proudly of wishing for someone to find her. You can probably hear the tune echoing in your head right now. *The Little Mermaid* gives up her family, her property, and her fins to live happily ever after with her prince.

Television and advertising are major culprits with unrelenting stereotypes of women. In the 1990's, *Beverly Hills 90210* had a huge audience of young people. The show's smartest character, Andrea, survived a crisis to become class valedictorian at Beverly Hills High. Then she goes off to study at college with a major in pre-medicine and get pregnant. She drops out of school so she can get a job to support the father of the baby while he finishes medical school. What's up with that?

A cable TV channel dedicated to women's programming shows one movie after another where the abused woman is rescued in the nick of time. These fantasies die hard and it takes a long time. The rescue myth says that we shouldn't have to learn about money, that someone will do it for us.

On the other extreme are women who are overwhelmed by family responsibilities and who think that superwoman is the standard. Plagued by the immediate crises of financial burden, a sense of over-responsibility keeps the focus on solving the problems of now. There isn't the time, energy or additional resources to look toward the future, much less prepare for it.

WI$DOM:
"If you don't know enough about management and finances, hire someone who does." — JULIA CHILD

The superwoman myth leaves us feeling ashamed to ask for help from anyone, and, often, too proud to accept help when it is offered. Superwomen are supposed to do it alone.

The "I can't" myth tells us just that. A lack of confidence impedes our competence in economic matters. Money is too much like math, and girls aren't supposed to be good at math. Money was always the father's territory. The "I can't" women were carefully taught at an early age that money was too complicated. We were not to worry our "pretty little heads about it" and that "husbands are supposed to take care of all that." At the other end of this spectrum are women who grew up in welfare families in welfare neighborhoods who learned to try and survive on that check. The "I can't" myth is particularly powerful and pervasive. James Stowers titled his book *Yes, You Can!* for just this reason.

$TATI$TIC:

Seven of 10 "Boomer" women will outlive their husbands. They can expect to be widows for 15 to 20 years.[19]

The magical thinking myth says it will all work out, somehow or other. We can just do whatever we want and somehow it will be okay. It is a little like Scarlett O'Hara's philosophy: think about it tomorrow.

We are all affected by these myths when it comes to money. We may also have our unique variations on these themes. We simply need to know what our belief system is so that it won't get in the way of learning what we need to know about money.

Here's another secret: anyone who wants to protect us from having to deal with money is not our friend. The so-called protection is crippling. We must learn and help other women to learn that it's only money.

Let's think about the women who came before us — our mothers and grandmothers. Let's talk about what were their lives were like? Have things changed financially for them? Have they adapted well or not? Pay attention to the concepts about money and work that they taught you. Was money above or beneath you, out of your reach, unfathomable, or highly desirable? What do you want money to mean in your life?

Our Moneyworks is humming along. It's only money, it's only money, it's only money.

RESOURCES:

Women have been writing about money for many years. Read a great book: *Sense and Sensibility* or any Jane Austen novel; *Middlemarch* by George Eliot; *Little Women* by Louisa May Alcott; or a modern memoir, *Dreaming: Hard Luck and Good Times in America,* by Carolyn See.

7. Risky Business: Debt vs. Freedom

Ever have one of those moments when something that was foggy or unknown becomes crystal clear? Freud described that moment as an "Aha" experience. Oftentimes, we will say exactly that: Aha.

I had one of those moments last night watching an interview of Henry Chu, an American-born, ethnic Chinese journalist stationed in Beijing. He talked about the numbers of American name brands now appearing in China, and the vast markets opening up there. He described the wads of cash that people carry to pay for their purchases, large and small. Margaret Warner of PBS's *News Hour* made a comment about China not being a consumer society. Chu corrected her by saying that it is, indeed, a major consumer culture but not a consumer credit culture; cash is the currency, not plastic.

Aha! In the last half of the 20th century, America became not just a consumer society, but a consumer credit society. We are encouraged to buy things that we can't pay for. When was the last time you saw a customer pay cash for a refrigerator or a computer or a car? It's even rare to see someone use cash at the supermarket. Yes, some people do write checks, and those are mainly cash-based. But think about it: when was the last time you saw someone write a check to buy a refrigerator or a car?

$TATI$TIC:

Women spend 85% of the consumer dollar.[20]

Most Americans are drowning in debt; that's the price for having all of the stuff that we have. If we had to save up and pay cash for what we think we have to have, we wouldn't have some of our stuff. Imagine what that would be like. What would the advertisers do with themselves?

Not to mention the banks; they are thriving on the debt of consumers. Banks earn somewhere between 10% and 25% on our debt — that is quite a payoff. And today, our debt can start really early. As the 21st century begins, not only college students, but also high school students, are recruited to the plastic brigade.

Women over 50 will remember a time when there was no such thing as Master Card or Visa. Elder women will remember a time when there was no such thing as credit. For younger women, bank credit cards are commonplace. Not only is it hard to imagine not having them, they have become a necessity in the computerized world in which we live. However, credit card debt can put us off-balance before we realize it.

In the record store where I spent much of my childhood, everything was cash and carry, as it was in most businesses. If you bought a 45 rpm record, you paid 89 cents plus tax — no other options. If you didn't have the money, you didn't get the record. Department stores had charge accounts as they still do today, but there were no generic credit cards to be used from one store to another. It was much more difficult to spend money that you didn't have.

Things have changed immensely in the past few decades. It is almost impossible to find a place where you cannot use a credit card instead of cash. Credit cards can pay for your groceries, haircuts, gasoline, almost anything that your heart desires. Nowadays, it is very easy to spend money that you don't have; in fact, we are encouraged to spend money that we don't have — and that's a big problem.

WI$DOM:

"I carry travelers' checks which helps me to spend more wisely and eliminates overuse of my credit cards. I seem to be more frugal and end up walking away from an item that I probably didn't need. I also like to purchase US Savings Bonds for my children." — NELL CARTER

My friend Saralie talked about her first charge account. She got it when was 16 years old and working in a ski resort. She had escaped from a rigid father, a missionary in a remote area of Canada who firmly believed in the evil of sparing the rod. She took off and has never gone back.

So, at 16, Saralie was in a department store wishing that she could have an outfit that she loved. Her friend told her that she could open an account, and she did. She was thrilled. She picked out a number of outfits over the next few weeks, each time asking them to put it on her account. She remembers thinking how great it was that this store let you take things home without paying for them.

Naïve though she was at 16 and out in the world for the first time, she learned fast. Thirty days later, the bill arrived and she was shocked, and scared to death. Aha! She realized that she had charged more money than she could earn in a month. Right then, at 16, she learned not to spend money she didn't have. Even to this day, she uses plastic only when it is required. Her advice to women is to get an education and stay out of debt. In her mind, education = income and no debt = independence.

Debt and freedom balance like a seesaw; when one goes up, the other goes down. Debt is a very tricky issue in today's society. No matter how much or how little money in a family, we're all supposed to have a television; first it was black and white, then color, now HDTV, and soon flat screen. In the 1950's, the American consumer learned to buy a new car every 2 years.

Worse than the fashion industry's seasonal changes, technology actually forces us to move up — whether we can afford it or not. You can't buy vinyl records anymore except in quasi-antique stores and cassette tapes are *passé* we must have a CD player. As soon as everyone has a CD player, something new will replace it, forcing us to upgrade again.

And how do we do all of this? Plastic! A math professor in San Francisco lectures his college students on the perils of credit card debt. He calls credit cards the new slavery: if you become indebted, it can take a lifetime to get out and some people may never get free.

I wonder if he realizes that it is already too late for some of his students?

$TATI$TIC:

In 1998, 60% of college students had credit cards; 21% had more than 4 credit cards.[21]

I know an older couple with a horrifying story illustrating the nightmares of credit card debt. The husband had retired and the wife was having a terrible time adjusting. He was delighted to be home, managing the house now instead of the business, and she was going nuts. This is not such an unusual story: a lot of couples have a difficult period of adjustment to retirement.

However, she had a big secret: she had accumulated a massive debt over the course of their marriage. She was terrified that he would find out. He was happily reviewing their investments, making changes here and there, very pleased with their financial security. Meanwhile, she ran to get the mail each day, so she could hide the bills before he found them. She would spend hours each day trying to figure out how to juggle all of these accounts. For years, she had been taking new cards and using credit card checks to make payments on the older debts. He started to get suspicious that something was wrong, maybe that she was having an affair.

The history of this traditional marriage was a longstanding

power struggle over many things, including how the money was to be spent. Every time the husband vetoed a purchase for one of their daughters, she charged it to one of these secret credit cards. Much of this debt was many, many years old. She had been paying the minimum payments, meaning interest only, for all those years; the interest alone now amounted to $20,000 per year.

She was about to break under the pressure of her secret debt, and her husband was still blithely unaware of any financial problems. He had been a high-level executive who, clearly, never wanted to know about her money problems. When we think about it, it must have taken quite a bit of denial over the years to not notice that all the purchases he had vetoed appeared anyway.

Many months later, she finally told him, but only when she was so overwhelmed by her secret that she couldn't take it anymore. For his part, once he knew, his major concern was the emotional toll these secret debts had cost her. He understood that he had been a passive participant in this debt.

The irony is that he had always insisted that his junior executives get a copy of their credit reports each year to make sure there were no errors, but he had never accessed his own credit report. If he had, he would have learned about these secret accounts years earlier, and saved them a lot of grief and money.

This story had a happy ending. This couple had substantial investments and the entire debt was paid within days. They repented their respective roles in this drama, and now they are enjoying retirement and each other in a way they never have before — and with no more interest payments.

Not all stories about debt have such a happy ending. Some of us don't even want to know what our debt story is, thinking that if we don't know about it, it'll go away. Maybe we think that we'll never get out of debt anyway, so we don't look; it'll just make us more miserable.

$TATI$TIC:

One of 3 women with both savings and credit cards owes more on credit cards than she has in her retirement account.[22]

Let me talk for a minute about credit reports. There was a time when I didn't even know these existed; it was a shock to learn that my every financial move was tracked. Three large companies (Equifax, Trans Union, and Experian/TRW) follow every account we have. These companies keep records of the amounts that we owe and our payment history on each account.

This happens to every one of us, whether we like it or not. Every time we apply for a credit card, a student loan, or a car loan, we must give our Social Security number. Our financial history is accessed through that number, again whether we like it or not.

If we pay a bill late, or miss a payment, or even worse, default on any debt, that information is tracked by the credit reporting agencies. Negative information, which stays on the report for seven years if it is accurate, can cost us higher rates or even prevent us from getting a credit card, a new car, or a home loan. Our mistakes get us a 7-year sentence, whether we like it or not.

Of course, if we have only positive information on our credit report, that is a very good sign to banks and other lenders. We qualify much more easily for a car loan or home loan if our report is excellent. Ever heard the complaint that banks will only lend money to people who don't really need it?

In addition to our credit report, we actually receive a grade, a credit score, by an agency called Fair, Issacs and Company — it's called a FICO score. In the 20th century, this score was a closely guarded secret available only to banks and other lenders. One of the early miracles of the 21st century is that individuals are now allowed access to our own FICO scores on the internet. Of course, we have to pay for them — hmm, big surprise — with a credit card.

The good thing is that, with a computer, it's really easy to do. It used to be a drag to write the credit reporting agencies and wait 3-4 weeks to receive the report in the mail. Now we can get our FICO score and a credit report from Equifax in about a minute and a half. At this point, it costs us $12.95 to access our information and I imagine they are rolling in the dough. I think it ought to be free, but I also think banks shouldn't be charging 24% interest to their poorest clients.

Anyway, to do this, go online to www.myfico.com, click on Score Power, and give some information and a credit card number. Abracadabra! The credit report from Equifax and the FICO score will appear on your screen. Scores can range from 300 to 850, the higher the better.

They will explain how they arrived at the score and what changes would make it higher. If there are late payments any time in the past 7 years, if the balances are too close to the credit limit, and/or if there are too many account balances, the score will be lower than if everything is perfect. Only scores over 700 begin to qualify for those low-interest rates we keep hearing about.

Sometimes, there are errors on these credit reports. It may contain information about someone else's accounts if the name is fairly common, or it may list an incorrect delinquency, or other error. There is a way to have items investigated online or we can contact them by phone, FAX, or mail. In fact, the credit reporting agencies are good about correcting any errors. If you find an error, make sure to check with all three agencies for corrections because they don't seem to talk to each other.

$TATI$TIC:

Women are prime candidates for higher points and fees on mortgage applications.[23]

Ever get one of those pre-approved letters in the mail that guarantees a low, low rate only to be turned down or given a different card at a much higher rate? Does it make more sense now? Credit companies throw out a wide net with these solicitations, asking only for a Social Security number (Aha!) and a signature. Then they go look at the FICO scores of the applicants. If we really need a low interest rate to help us get out from under, we're probably not going to get it.

This brings me back to how the money management books don't work for us — yet. The people who write these books are on a different plane, in a different reality, than we are. Money managers tell us to make a list of all our outstanding debts and to begin to pay them off one at a time starting with the highest interest rate accounts first, blah, blah, blah. We went blank way back there and don't hear another word they say, but they keep talking.

They tell us to go to our parents or to the bank and get a no-interest or low-interest loan to pay off all of our debts. Gee, what a great idea! Why didn't we think of that? We didn't think of it because for most of us, those options don't exist.

To give the money managers their due, a few debtors (what a word!) have some of these options, but they haven't considered them because they are ashamed or paralyzed by their debts. For them, the money manager's suggestion is helpful. However, most of us don't have those avenues to freedom. It's a little harder than that for most of us.

To reinforce what I said earlier in this book, getting out of debt is the most important step toward freedom we can take. Knowing the details of our debt and talking about how to get out of debt are crucial. However, talking about debt also can be a humiliating experience, so we need to remember to take special care with each other.

If you don't have much debt, be grateful for your good fortune and try to not be too judgmental of others. People can get into debt for a lot of reasons; don't assume irresponsibility as the only cause. When you manage to get out of debt, be kind to others. I have known people who have paid off their debts, and become disdainful, even nasty, about friends who have debts. What's up with that? It's probably like those of us who can read looking down on those who can't.

Many people who get out of debt quickly have done it because of some kind of windfall — a large increase in income, a gift, an inheritance, or one of those no-interest loans. For most of us, getting out of debt will take a while. We may not like to hear it, but there it is.

Freedom from credit card debt is our goal. Remember that there are going to be individual differences in getting out of debt, too. One woman might be able to ask a parent for a gift; another may qualify for a bank loan to consolidate her debts as a reasonable interest rate. A woman with a large debt, damaged credit, and no family resources may simply have to increase payments a little bit each month for many years until she is debt-free. Each debt paid will give us a little more freedom. Let's go for it!

Try this. It's nitty, gritty time: time to talk about our debt and our credit reports. No matter how bad it is, it isn't impossible, and especially with a little help from our friends. If you can't stand to look at how much you owe yet, look at how many accounts you have. That'll do for the moment. If you feel brave, have access to a computer, and don't mind spending the $12.95, you might want to get your FICO score and your credit report, particularly if you've never seen it. And remember: it's only money.

RESOURCES:

If you're ready to get out of debt, the best advisor in the world is Mary Hunt. Her story, which is dynamite, led her to found the Cheapskate Monthly Newsletter. She is a real person who has written a couple of books that are down-to-earth and really helpful. Her Web site used to be pretty basic and totally non-threatening; now it's more elaborate, but still has really good information at www.cheapskatemonthly.com. There is a cost to subscribe, but I think it's worth every penny.

Go to womentalkmoney.com to tell your story and to read other women's stories about credit reports, getting out of debt, spending, saving, and earning.

8. Row, Row, Row Your Boat Down the Income Streams

errily debt-free, our life would be a dream. Our income would go a lot further, too. With more income and a plan, we could be debt-free. So, let's talk about generating income, how to increase our income, and the concept of income streams.

As I said earlier, the 20th century saw women generating income as never before with the biggest push during the 40's and after the 60's. The Crash of 1929 also forced some middle- and upper-middle-class women to earn money for the first time.

The Great Depression was an economic phenomenon that, I hope, future generations will never encounter. It ruined many families and led to bread lines, widespread poverty, and suicides. If you have parents, grandparents, or great-grandparents who lived during the 1930's, you will see still the effects that the "Crash" had on them. Many of them have a wariness of the stock market and the banks that survives seventy years later. My aunt still saves the juice from canned vegetables to use in her soups.

Remember the movie *Auntie Mame*? That story was based on the life of a wild and wealthy woman who lived during those times. The butler announces the Crash when he tells Mame that her stockbroker wants to speak to her before he jumps out of the window. A series of hilarious and poignant scenes portray her attempts at jobs as an actress, receptionist, and retail clerk until Beauregard Jackson Pickett Burnside, her Prince Charming, arrives from his oil fields to rescue her. It was not so glamorous for most women of that time.

My maternal grandmother was a lovely Southern woman whose family had homes in Alabama and Maryland, and a summer home in Virginia. She was one of four perfectly coiffed and mani-cured sisters whose garden parties and teas were chronicled in the Birmingham *News*. My grandmother never dreamed that she would be a working woman, but the Depression sent her into the May Company department store to support not just herself, but three children and her 60-year old father who had never worked a day in his life.

Thank goodness, Julia had a great sense of humor and she was grateful to have a job during those tough years. She had managed to keep the butler, who also cooked, because he needed a place to live, but the cleaning help had to be let go. One afternoon, my mother, who was then a teenager, found my grandmother scrub-bing the bathroom floor with her manicured hands. Julia looked up and laughed, saying, "Oh, how the mighty have fallen."

Today's reality is that most women will have to generate income at some point during their lifetimes. Up to two-thirds of mothers of young children work at least part-time to help meet their families' expenses. In fact, experts tell us that, with the increased life expectancy, we may have three or four different careers over a lifetime. Studies indicate that continued stimulation from work and other interests helps brain activity in the elderly. It's good for us to have work and it helps to have extra money in the family. So, if generating income is good for us, what is the problem?

WI$DOM:

"The most important advice about money that I would give women today is to spend less than you earn and save for retirement. Today, many of America's women face a retirement without economic security. Less than a third of all female retirees have pensions, and the majority of those that do receive less than $5,000 a year. Younger women may not be earning the pension benefits they think they are, and older women are losing the pension benefits they thought they had.

To make sure that the 'golden years' are not the 'disposable years,' women need to take charge of their own retirement. The first step is to protect pension benefits by following the 'Pension 8'.*If you spend less than you earn and follow these eight steps, you are well on your way to a secure retirement."

— FORMER SENATOR CAROL MOSELEY-BRAUN

* See Appendix A

Too many women are working in dead-end jobs. Some women are just marking time until they get married; then, things will be magically different. (We'll talk about economics in relationships in the next chapter.) Right now, let's focus on women and work in the 21st century.

A couple of years ago, Leslie Stahl did a story about women and welfare — a hot topic at the time. These welfare mothers were being counseled, so-called, into clerical and service jobs that paid a minimum wage, kept them away from their children all day, gave them little if any health benefits, and offered no opportunities for advancement. Gee, what a bargain! I wonder why more women weren't rushing to sign up?

As Stahl wisely pointed out, they could just as easily have been trained as programmers instead of word processors, or bricklayers instead of cleaning women. Why weren't they? We'd almost have to conclude that the powers-that-be do not want welfare women to prosper, but to stay in their place. The kind interpretation is that women's income is still seen as secondary or supplemental income — and that's a big roadblock for women who are supporting families.

$TATI$TIC:

An Alabama coal miner, the first woman in her mine, earned about $20,000 a year less than men with comparable experience.[24]

When I first started talking to women about money, friends would tell me that I just had to talk to their sister or cousin or friend about her experiences, and they were right. I have heard some great stories from these referrals. My friend Ron introduced me to Billie who defines work as having fun and making money — not the definition of work for most people. Billie had to go through a transformation from Assistant VP to jewelry importer to get there.

Billie was a very bright girl who went to an Ivy League college and was one of only 10 women in her undergraduate class of 100. One of her first jobs was analyzing the cost-benefit of building a new plant. She had a great income that paid for her extensive vacations to exotic destinations, but she hated her job. Quite simply, her work didn't work for her.

WI$DOM:
"Do what you love and the $ will follow."
– OLYMPIA DUKAKIS

Although she tried to stick it out, she knew she needed to give it up and take a chance on what she really wanted to do. She wanted to combine travel with income; she went looking for items that she could import and sell in the States. She found a line of jewelry that she loved and started her own business. Like magic?

Billie didn't know the first thing about importing or sales, but she learned. She talked to people, read a lot, and started selling the jewelry to stores. She learned about discounts, invoicing, packaging, and shipping. She and a friend used to search for discarded boxes that she could re-use to save on shipping costs.

She worked hard and traveled hard; her business was a big success. She doesn't regret leaving that vice-presidency for a moment. Her advice to us is to make money at something you love. Now, her work works for her.

Having fun and making money would not be the definition of work for most people. Too often, work and fun are very separate experiences as, in fact, they were for Billie in the corporate setting. Now is a good time to start talking about how you make money. There are at least three questions to consider. Are you good at what you do? Do you enjoy what you do? Do you make enough money at it? In other words, does your work work for you?

Work is one of the two major problems that bring most people to therapy; love is the other one. As a psychotherapist, I have seen many people through issues of both work and love. The most worrisome situation is when someone is having trouble in both of these spheres; the extremely high level of stress is almost intolerable for more than a short period of time. Right now, let's focus on the work sphere; we'll talk about love later.

$TATI$TIC:

Women are chronically uninsured. Comparing men and women by hours worked, by job tenure, or by company size, women are less likely to receive health insurance from their employers.[25]

We know, although I will say it again, that most women will generate income to support ourselves, and our families. We also know that most women earn less than most men. From those facts, we can conclude that most women are at a bit of a disadvantage in the work sphere. How's that for an understatement? Given that, let's talk about the questions I asked about work, because our answers will determine whether or not we need to make a change.

Are you good at what you do? The first story that pops into my head is about my younger daughter's brief tenure as a waitress in an English tea shoppe. Her sister, two years older, was having a great time working there after school; she loved the tips. When a position opened up, Julianna applied. She was a sweet, personable waitress. Remembering the orders was no problem, but something about the balancing act eluded her; she had several accidents a week sending teapots and cups crashing to the floor. She would come home and say, "You'll never believe it. I did it again." She went on to other after-school jobs at which she did very well. She never tried waiting tables again.

If you've never thought about this, think about it now. It's an important question. Are you good at what you do? Does it match your skills and your temperament?

Do you enjoy what you do? You may have the most resistance to this question, or you may think that I am slightly crazy for raising it. I believe that our work needs to be something that we enjoy, perhaps not rollicking fun every minute, but something that we like to do and from which we derive satisfaction.

Since I work with many artists and writers, I find that most of my clients can answer affirmatively to the first two questions: they are good at their work and they enjoy it. Making enough money is sometimes a problem.

However, I have worked with a number of women in law who are very good at what they do and who make more than enough money, but who, nevertheless, do not enjoy their work. Actually, it is often not the work itself but the requirements of the work setting which include extremely long hours, intense pressure to bill a minimum number of hours each month, and the highly aggressive and competitive nature of big law firms.

$TATI$TIC:

In 1960, 5.8% of women had 4 years or more of college; in 1992, 18.6%.[26]

If you are not enjoying your work, take a good look at what you don't like about it and figure out what the options are. While some women leave law, for example, to work in other fields, others opt out of the partnership race, develop flex-time schedules to accommodate their personal lives, job-share, or go into solo practice. As you talk about your work, try and get clear about what you might like to change if you could.

Do you make enough money? "Enough" money is a relative term, and only you can answer this question. What is enough for you may be very different from what is enough for someone else. If you make enough money and you like your work, you're in great shape. If you don't, it's time to talk about how that can change. Making enough money is critical to our present and our future.

If you like your work and you're good at it, but it doesn't make you enough money, can you be paid more? Women are not great at asking for a raise or negotiating a better deal — and the marketplace is aware of that. A negative response about getting a raise sounds like an absolute to many women. Sometimes, we won't even ask because we don't want to hear a negative answer.

Here's another secret: WE DON'T GET WHAT WE DON'T ASK FOR, mostly. So, get ready to ask for what you want and then negotiate for a little more than the company is willing to give you. WHAT? It's called negotiating.

For some reason, men learn negotiating skills but many women don't. Well, girls, it's time to learn. Negotiation is just a game with certain rules. If you ask for a 15% raise and they offer you 5%, pause for a moment. Offer back with a 12% compromise. Here's a quick lesson in negotiating skills.

Always ask for more than you really want: that's rule #1. The company will assume that you have done just that. They will offer you about half of what you asked for, saying that it is the best they can do: that's rule #2. Rule #3: you make a counteroffer closer to your original request. They complain, give a little more, and say that it is the absolute best they can do: rule #4. You can play this through one more time, if you aren't sweating those Carolyn See bullets by then, or you can stop at that point and say, "Thank you."

WI$DOM:
"SAVE IT!"   — JOAN FONTAINE

If you ask for a raise and get a flat refusal, you might want to think about changing companies, changing fields, going back to school, or starting your own business. Obviously, the last two choices require a little ready capital that you may not have. (We'll talk about cushions later.) As Lord Byron said, "Ready money is Aladdin's lamp."

Anyway, unless you have a plan, like a lot of backup or another job waiting for you, avoid the impulse to quit on the spot and storm out the door. Try to negotiate, but if that doesn't work, you have to face the fact that you are at a dead end in this job — time to look around.

I talked with an executive recruiter in Santa Barbara who is convinced that sales is a great career for women; it provides flexibility and the potential for high earnings. Since sales is about personal contact and building a relationship with customers, Carol thinks it's a good fit for many women. No, she doesn't mean working in retail for an hourly wage; she's talking about selling products, like pharmaceuticals or cellular phones or paper, in the field and for a commission.

Carol had been a single mom working for an employment company. She realized she needed more income to get ahead and buy a home, so she asked for a raise. She got a flat negative, and took the big risk of going out on her own. She didn't have a lot of money saved, but she did have a cousin who was willing to back her up if she needed some money. She was a great success. She's still doing what she likes and what she's good at, but now she's making more than enough money.

Given the corporate glass ceiling that women keep bumping their heads on, many women are choosing to start their own businesses. Women-owned businesses are now the largest growing segment of employment for women. Many women who are owners hire other women; sounds like our Moneyworks in action.

$TATI$TIC:

Women-owned businesses account for $2.28 trillion in annual sales.[27]

If it's not realistic for you to change jobs now, and if you can't get a significant raise, then you may want to think about a second income. Not another job?! No, I'm not talking about another job, but about something that you like to do that could earn you a little more money.

Cheryl Broussard, a financial planner who doesn't talk over

our heads, talked with me about how common cottage industries used to be. Women would make some extra money by baking, sewing, ironing, knitting, or making things at home in their spare time. As a little girl, Cheryl sold handmade headbands at school. She'd like to see women bring back the practice of cottage industries. Her advice to us is to "bring in more money and get clear about what the money will accomplish." She is a big believer in goals.

Now that we've talked about generating income, let's talk about income streams. The first time I heard the term, income streams, was from Phoebe Beasley, a truly fine artist. If you know her work, you know what I mean; if not, you're in for a grand experience. Her portraits of grandmothers are particularly haunting. Her work is collected internationally and by famous Americans including Oprah, Bill Russell, and Maya Angelou to name only a few.

I had an incredible opportunity to talk with Phoebe about women and money. She outlined an array of her projects: a limited edition book of the work of Langston Hughes with Maya Angelou; a gallery show; a poster for the LA Marathon; art for the 2000 Presidential election; a design for a sport shoe, and artwork for the re-launching of the Amistad. Phoebe is a very busy woman. She said, "You must have income streams. Because the world is so tentative now, you cannot depend on money from only one source. You must never rely on any one person for your support."

The concept of income streams was so clear to me that it had immediate appeal. Something just struck a chord for me. The term may have been around, but I had not been open to it. In fact, it was exactly what I was in the midst of creating for myself, but I had not thought about it consciously. It had a name: income streams.

Since I am trained as a psychologist, the notion of consciousness is very important to me. That is what we work toward in psychotherapy. Often, unconscious information gets in our way and we behave in ways that are not useful; consciousness is the goal. But sometimes, our unconscious, like in our dreams, leads us right where we need to go.

WI$DOM:

"Start a pension plan — at an early age!!"
— FANNIE FLAGG

I had been moving in the direction of income streams, but without a conscious plan. I had finished the manuscript for this book. I was beginning to work on my Web site, continuing to work in my practice, and trying to make a few more days available for writing and talks. The result would be four income streams, yet I had never heard the concept. My unconscious process, some might call it intuition, had been leading me in the right direction.

Let's talk about how income streams could improve your life. We all have at least one income stream, whatever it may be. How many do you have? How solid is your set of income streams? Is your survival totally dependent on another person? How stable is that relationship? Is your income dependent on your job? What if you couldn't work? Is it dependent on a pension and, if so, how solid is that pension fund? Is your future as an elderly woman dependent on Social Security?

Whatever your situation, talk about ways to add both more income streams and more dependable income streams. You won't have to wander around like I did; you can figure out a plan and set your goals to get those income streams flowing.

Oops, I just thought of another song title: "We're in the Money." In *Gold Diggers of 1933*, Ginger Rogers sings it in pig Latin, a kind of backwards slang that was popular at the time.

RESOURCES:

Watch a great movie about money. Jane Austen's books have been appearing in very successful screen versions. Look for *Sense and Sensibility, Persuasion,* or *Pride and Prejudice. Norma Rae, Places in the Heart,* and *A Woman of Independent Means* are all movies tackling issues of women and money at one level or another; Sally Field stars in all three of them.

9. Some Day My Prince Will Come

P rince Charming was the fantasy for generations of women and for good reason: women were completely dependent on the men in their lives for their financial survival. When women weren't allowed to generate income, or own property, or inherit assets, some version of Prince Charming was an absolute necessity. Buy why is he such an enduring wish for women today?

Hmmm, let's see: tall, dark, good-looking, rich, charming, great dancer, beautiful house. I wonder why the wish endures? The 19th and 20th century novels and movies are filled with variations on Prince Charming: Mr. Darcy, Mr. Rochester, Rhett Butler, Nick Charles, Han Solo, the Prince from *Cinderella* or *Sleeping Beauty* or *Snow White*, and hundreds of others. It may be formulaic, but it works.

The 21st century version of Prince Charming would be a hip, quirky anti-hero type guy with a scruffy beard. Ideally, however, he still has to have the goods: tall, dark, good-looking, rich, great house, charming. Many young women spend most of their income trying to look pretty, so she can meet up with a guy who will fix it all. Is this progress?

Cheryl Broussard never had a fantasy about Prince Charming and understands the power of emotions when it comes to money. She would call the Prince an emotional trap. She firmly believes that we cannot benefit from financial experts like her as long as our emotions prevent us from understanding money.

I have asked a lot of women about Prince Charming. Many women of all ages are still looking. Others have called it a nice fantasy, but just that — a dream. A couple of happily married women have told me they have found their Prince. A number of women told me that they thought they had found the Prince, but were shocked by the subsequent reality of their lives.

My friend J thinks that there's an ethnic difference: that African American women are not raised with the Prince Charming fantasy. She may be right. I spoke to an African American entrepreneur whose mother worked as a maid to support her children. Her mother told her repeatedly, "You are your Prince Charming." Today, this woman spends her spare time preparing inner-city teens for their first jobs.

For many young women who grew up in financially comfortable homes, the transition into adulthood is rocky. They expect to be able to continue to live at the level of their parents, but they are earning entry-level salaries. Their frustration with the downturn in their life styles and their desire for more can fuel the princely wishes.

One young woman, who had grown up with travel, country

clubs, and a summer home at the lake, had never experienced money problems before. Of course, she had never been on her own before either. As a professional living in a very expensive city, she was frustrated by what she could not afford to do. Then she met a handsome young man with a high income and a significant trust fund; he could afford everything she wanted in life. It seemed too good to be true. The 3-carat engagement ring was stunning, but the flaws in the relationship became clear as the months went on. He simply didn't treat her very well, but giving up all the "perqs" really hurt.

WI$DOM:

"You need to invest, yes in the stock market, but also into yourself. You need to invest in education, extra classes if you need specific expertise. You should invest in the best wardrobe your money can afford. Make sure your appearance really shows the world who you are (or want to become). Invest in everything that makes you happy, because life is not a dress rehearsal, we're only here once so enjoy it as much as you can." — IVANA TRUMP

Meanwhile back at the ranch, so to speak, she had been working with a great guy who clearly cared for her, but whose economic prospects were less than dazzling. He came from a poor family, had a fair amount of debt, and a little non-princely weight on him. He had a few business losses, mainly because he was too kind. She began to realize how happy she was when she was with him and how well he treated her, but he sure didn't look like Charming.

For many months, she resisted becoming involved with him mainly because of the economic factors. Finally, she told him about her concerns; she wanted them to build a solid financial base for their future family. Although it took some work on both their parts, today this couple is happily married with a successful business and a growing family.

$TATI$TIC:

Only 10% of black women and 8% of Latinas who are 65 or older have private pension income.[28]

For today's couples, money is the #1 cause of arguments, not to mention stress. Major conflicts exist in the expectations of women and men. Most women have jobs and support themselves when they are single, but many expect the spouse to be the major provider after marriage, and, often, the sole provider after a baby is born. Many men, on the other hand, have grown up around working women and expect relationships to be income-generating partnerships. These guys don't even like Prince Charming, and they certainly never wanted to have to *be* the Prince.

Granted, there are men who are the sole providers, there are women who manage on their own, and there are couples who work together to generate the family resources. The critical component is agreement. If both parties agree that one person is to be the moneymaker, and they are both happy with that, great. Obviously, he or she has to be able to make enough money to do that.

The arguments start when the members of a couple have differing ideas about who is supposed to make the money and how much. When one person expects the other to make all the money, but the other cannot make enough or doesn't want to do it alone, there will be major problems in the relationship.

Mind you, it isn't always the woman who has the expectations of being supported. I know a woman who married a man who didn't make as much money as she. It was a big problem for her: she didn't want to have a junior partner for a husband. He agreed and promised to work harder.

After the marriage, not only did he not make more money, he stopped working altogether and made it clear that he didn't want to work. He said that she made enough money for both of them, and, since she liked to work and he didn't, he couldn't see what the problem was. They are now divorced. Because California is a community property state, she had to buy out his share of the house even though her income had paid for it; and she makes a hefty alimony payment to him each month.

Another young woman I know lost her job just after she was married and hasn't been able to find another one yet. Her new husband is trying to be supportive, but he is not happy about it, even though he earns more than enough money for their needs. His position is that she is a young, smart, "able-bodied" woman with an advanced degree, and she ought to be contributing to the household. They are, however, agreed that when they have children, she will be a stay-at-home mom. Until then, he wants her to earn money.

$TATI$TIC:

In a study, 88% of high school students said they learned everything they know about money from their parents.[29]

There are those old horror stories where the wife works in a menial job to put her husband through medical school and, then, once he is a successful physician, she no longer fits his ideal and he wants a divorce. Of course, the jilted corporate wife has the nightmare of having suppressed her own career to be a partner in her husband's executive life. She helps him rise to the top of his company only to be discarded and to hear him say that it's his money, because he earned it. These are cases of bargains that changed and, in many of these cases, the woman is short-changed.

Things do alter over the course of many years and couples have to be able to adapt to those changes — physical, emotional, and financial. Those who do not adapt will separate, or be miserable together.

In the marriage of a colleague, they had both decided that she would be at home and he would generate the money. However, over the years, she became bitter, saying that he didn't make enough money, and that he worked too many hours. He tried to make more money, but then he was working 60 hours a week, and she was even angrier.

Many years into this bargain, when the kids were in high school, he was tired. Finally, he was diagnosed with cancer. It was a wake-up call for him. He asked his wife to pursue her Ph.D., or start a small business, or work in her pre-marriage career — just part-time — enough to help a little and prepare for the time when the kids would leave for college. She was outraged and immovable. I tried to talk to her about it. Her therapist told her it was time to begin helping him with the financial burden. She stopped talking to me, and she stopped seeing the therapist. Honestly, I had thought that she would change her mind, but I was wrong. This couple is divorced now.

Knowing your expectations about generating income after marriage, or if you become a stay-at-home mom, will avoid a lot of conflicts. I cringe when people say that an at-home mom isn't working; that is probably the hardest work of all, even though it doesn't earn any money. Most experts would agree that babies and little children are best served by having as much contact as possible with their parents.

Today's economics won't support a stay-at-home mom for many families, but affordable childcare is in short supply. Enough is enough! Childcare and that 30% income disparity are two major domestic problems to be solved in the 1st decade of the 21st century.

In general, I think generating income is a good idea for adults, whether female or male, no matter what age, in a relationship or not, whether or not they have a trust fund. We need to make a contribution to society. Most women would not expect their partners to carry them around on their backs all day. Why would we expect to be carried financially? Having an income increases our sense of self-esteem, keeps us young, helps us to be independent, and equalizes the power dynamics in a relationship.

WI$DOM:

"Marry for love — never for financial security." – CHRISTINE BARANSKI

Here are two secrets about love and relationships. A good relationship is a partnership with shared values and honest, loving treatment — no matter who makes the money. The second secret about love is to feel the behavior, not the words. What someone does to you, or with you, is much more bankable than what they tell you they're going to do. When it comes to love and money, it is crucial to pay attention to the difference between words and behavior.

Words can be dangerous emotional traps for women. "I'm sorry." "I didn't mean to." "I want you to be happy." "I'll change." "I'll never do it again." "We only want the best for you." "I don't ever want you to have to worry about money." How many times have we gotten caught in words like these? When it comes to money and love, behavior determines the future, whether in intimate relationships or family. Let's look at a few examples.

A young woman with an MBA developed a product that was highly successful and suddenly had an influx of income beyond what she had ever imagined. Her father, who was so proud of her, wanted to advise her on investment strategies. Her ideas were different from her father's, but she loved him and took his advice. She lost all her money. How could this have happened?

She had failed to look at her father's behavior. He had lost not one, but two fortunes by making poor investment decisions. The good news is that she learned from her mistake and, when she had her next success, she made the investment decisions. She still loves her father; she just can't take his advice on money.

Another hard-working young woman, who had grown up in a very poor family, was dating a privileged young man, a real prince. He would say repeatedly that he wanted to take care of her, but his behavior was far from that. His words were so powerful to her that she would, time and again, overlook the reality or excuse it. He would say that he wanted to take her shopping, then he would buy expensive items for himself, but he could never seem to find anything he thought was suitable for her. When they would plan an evening out, he would ask her what she wanted to do, and then suggest the opposite.

$TATI$TIC:
Women are 47% of multiple-job holders.[30]

She finally realized that she could only count on him to let her down. She had threatened to break up with him. He begged her to let him take her out to lunch so they could talk; she agreed, hoping yet again that he would come through for her. First, he asked her to pick him up; then, he forgot his wallet, and asked her to pay the check, promising that he would pay her back. After she had paid the check, he laughed and thanked her for taking him out to lunch. Obviously, he was a jerk and she was conflicted about being treated well, but I have seen too many women focus on the romantic words in spite of what is actually happening in the relationship.

Here is one last story of words vs. behavior. A 40-ish woman decided to live with the love of her life, who had a great deal more money than she. Eventually, they decided to buy a house together. Her love made the down payment, and, since they were not married, the house was put in the love's name. This woman paid half the mortgage, half the maintenance costs, and half of all other expenses with the understanding that they were partners. Together, they had decided that 50-50 was equal, even though it took 90% of her income to be equal vs. 30% of love's income to be equal. Hear the problem?

During the 10 years that they were together, she asked a few times that love add her name to the deed, but there was always some reason that this couldn't happen. No great surprise to us, she woke up one day to find that her love had fallen for another woman. She lost her love, her home, and her so-called investment. She had listened to the words.

Eliza Doolittle's refrain has to be ours also: "Show Me". People who love us treat us well. People who love us work with us, not above us or against us. People who love us don't need to control or dominate us financially; they don't want to protect us from learning about money.

Take some time to analyze your relationships, past and present. Talk about your emotional traps when it comes to love and money. What have you learned from past relationships with intimates and family members?

The way we love and are loved will affect our financial future. People who love us want us to do well, and they help us to learn what we need to know. After all, it's only money.

RESOURCES:

Relationships are all around you — dating relationships, marriages, parent-child and other familial relationships, relationships with bosses and co-workers. Observe them carefully.

A Woman of Independent Means by Elizabeth Forsythe Hailey is a great book to read at this point.

10. A Pocketful of Miracles:
Bag Ladies and Other Crises

Pocketful of Miracles is an old movie starring Bette Davis as a bag lady who sells apples on the street corner. Fallen from grace due to the "drink," she is a neighborhood fixture. As I remember it, her crisis comes in the form of a letter announcing the impending arrival of her daughter (!) from finishing school (?!) in Europe. Apple Annie becomes hysterical; she doesn't want her daughter to see her like this. I would think she'd be delighted that she didn't have to pay for finishing school any more; that tuition money could buy her some pretty good digs. It was Hollywood in the 50"s, what can I say?

Anyway, the men who own a nightclub on the block help her out. The guys do the "gee, she-cleans-up-pretty-good" routine transforming Annie into a middle-aged lady who graciously receives and entertains the young girl, played by Ann-Margret, no less. All's well that ends well. The guys feel good, Annie is grateful, the girl is happy. We won't begin to go into how many things are wrong with this picture; as I said, it was Hollywood.

WI$DOM:

"Get yourself the best financial advisor you can afford. Go over every "piece" of money you own now, or will in the future. Money includes cash, investments, real estate, jewelry, etc. PLAN AS EARLY AS YOU CAN for the future for yourself and your children." — IVANA TRUMP

The end of the 20th century found too many people living on the streets and begging for subsistence — some people say it's a scam. All I can say is, if I were going to pick a scam, I'd prefer one where I didn't have to carry a bag of belongings and not bathe for weeks at a time. Fewer women than men seem to be on the street, and even fewer mothers with children, but they are found in every city.

How do bag ladies get to that point? Complex disabling combinations of mental illness and substance abuse are probable causes, but some have, or see, no other options. The very old women are the saddest to me.

Striking to me is when I hear a woman say that she is afraid of becoming a bag lady. Paradoxically, I have only heard this fear voiced by unlikely candidates: women from the middle and upper-middle class who have substantial assets. Frankly, I don't get it. I can understand fearing poverty and not having enough money, because that is the best prediction for many women. But bag ladies?

At first, I thought the bag lady fear was limited to women who had not worked outside the home and had always been dependent on someone else for their support. That would make a little more sense to me because survival is externalized. I have had, let us say, strong discussions with women who have million dollar homes, retirement accounts, savings, and wealthy parents who have firmly held their ground that they could be bag ladies at any moment. If you have this phobia, I want you to take a good look at it and see if you can get past it. As my compassionate friend Steve always says, "Get over it."

The problem is that phobias paralyze us. Contrary to my original thoughts, women who are high-earners and independent, in many ways, may also share the fear of being bag ladies. If it weren't so terrifying for them, it would be funny.

$TATI$TIC:

By 1990, women represented 44% of economists, 27% of lawyers, 38% of pharmacists, 22% of doctors, and 30% of stockholders.[31]

Picture a woman who owns a successful company. She negotiates deals every day, she is really savvy with money, and she thinks that she will be a bag lady. She has been saving money since she was a little girl, started putting money into retirement accounts years ago, and owns two houses. What's up with that?

I wonder if the bag lady phobia is attached to some early trauma of abandonment or shame? The fear is so powerful that it has a primitive feel to it. Many of us learn our money styles from our mothers. Perhaps these women picked up on their mother's anxiety when they were very little. I want to know if their mothers are bag ladies, or if they even know any bag ladies.

It may be fear of the unknown or fear of loss. I talked to a lawyer who thinks it's about having stuff: that if you don't have property or funds to lose, you don't worry about it. That makes sense, but still the reaction is pretty extreme. I wonder if those who have the bag lady fear could pare it down to size: fear that

they may not have the big house or the second house forever, rather than seeing themselves on the street. Maybe change of any sort is simply appalling.

Maybe they don't feel very strong, or they lack self-confidence in their abilities to weather a storm; maybe they just haven't had the experience yet. I have one more hypothesis, which is about the concept of enough money. It may be that they are not clear — <u>yet</u> — about what enough money is for them. They may think that more is always better and that there will never be enough.

I haven't talked to a single poor or working class woman who has this fear. That doesn't mean they don't exist, but I haven't talked to them. I think it possible that women who have had to struggle a lot or who have gotten through a particularly tough time have a different experience. If I apply that personally, it fits. I have definitely been through some tough times financially, but I have never worried about being a bag lady.

It may be a combination of experience and modeling. If you've never been financially challenged or strapped, you have no idea how to do it — at least, that would be the fear. Women who've been challenged financially know they can survive it. In my case, I have worked most of my life; I learned to run a cash register when I was eight years old. And, of course, I see my 83-year old mother working part-time still — and enjoying it.

I talked to a woman who had lived on the streets, when she was a young mother with a small baby, many years ago. She had grown up in a very respectable family in respectable Philadelphia. She married a dashing young man who had one problem; he verbally abused her. They were not a good match and had terrible fights. After the baby was born, he became physically violent. One day, frightened about escalating violence, she left taking only the baby and the clothes on her back.

Too ashamed to go to her parents, she could not tell them that she had left her husband. Divorce was a disgrace to the entire family in those days. For weeks, she managed to hide the facts. She tells poignant stories of their survival. The Philadelphia train station became their bath; she washed her little girl in the sink at the train station.

Eventually, one of her friends realized in horror that she was homeless. This friend and her husband insisted that Pearl come and live with them until she could get herself established. Pearl almost said, "No." She had never taken what she saw as charity. Her pride was blocking her from accepting the help. Thank goodness she had the baby or she might not have taken their help. Her friend took care of the baby while Pearl started generating income.

Pearl tells some great stories about making money and taking risks. She started the first dog-grooming business in Philadelphia and became a bit of a celebrity, making television appearances and catering to an upscale crowd. Each day, dogs would arrive in limousines for their appointments with the chauffeurs waiting patiently on the sidewalk outside the salon.

$TATI$TIC:

From 1988 to 1998, the median salary of baby boom women increased by 25%. The disparity between median salaries of these women and men their same age was 34%.[32]

She took a chance on buying a small parking lot in Atlantic City when the town was in ruin. "What the heck," she thought, "people always need a place to park their cars." Within two years, gambling made the Boardwalk into a boomtown and a casino bought that little parking lot; selling it set her up for life. In recent years, she has been buying up the units in her condominium complex when they become available. She's come a long way from that train station.

Accepting help is an extremely important skill to learn. Had it not been for her friends' offer of help and her willingness to accept that help, Pearl may not have made it. She used her friends' help as a bridge to a new life for her and her daughter. She worked very, very hard to build a business and was wildly successful at it. Pearl, who is both generous and truly understanding, was in a position later on to offer help to others in need, and she found it very gratifying. Giving back is an important rule of life, and money.

Help is a two-way street: offering help when it is needed and being able to accept help when necessary. The process can get hung up on either side. If there was a time in your life when you were in need of help, think about how that felt.

Right now, there are women you know who are struggling. It

may be an elderly neighbor whose house is in obvious need of repair, or a single mom who could use a manicure or a new dress, or a kid who would love a new pair of shoes, or even better, a computer for schoolwork. Would it be so terrible to help them out, particularly if you have a lot more than they do?

Women you don't know are struggling: the woman in the wheelchair in front of the Post Office or the woman sleeping in the park with her dog. Think about how you feel when you see one of these women, or when she asks you for help. When I see a woman who is living on the street, almost always an older woman or a woman with a child, I cannot deny them if I have money in my pocket. Something in their lives has gone terribly wrong and a lot in my life is right; it seems only fair that I respond, even if it's in a small way.

WI$DOM:

"Get yourself the best financial advisor you can afford. Go over every "piece" of money you own now, or will in the future. Money includes cash, investments, real estate, jewelry, etc. PLAN AS EARLY AS YOU CAN for the future for yourself and your children."— IVANA TRUMP

Betsy (Elizabeth Forsythe) Hailey became very interested in homelessness and took action. Her concern about the homeless grew into a novel about a woman trying to understand privilege and want. Then, she put her money and her efforts where her heart was. She and a group of friends organized a homeless shelter for mothers and children in Hollywood. Dedicated to short-term, practical intervention, the shelter helps women get jobs and homes, providing safe childcare while they make these efforts. The shelter is really helping.

I think businesses and professions need to help more too. Restaurants, a few retail stores, and movie theaters offer a senior discount. What about grocery stores? Many professionals have an ethical obligation to see some patients or clients on a *pro bono* basis: that means for free, or at greatly reduced fees. Not nearly enough doctors or lawyers or dentists or psychologists adhere to this ethic.

WI$DOM:

"The only value of money is to spend it. So spend it wisely. Make as much as you can, use it wisely and always give some away to those in need." — DR. JOYCELYN ELDERS

What about that 30% disparity; what if all employers increased women's wages by 30%? What a difference that would make! How about if all women over 75, or even 80, received a 30% increase in Social Security payments? Think of it as a real cost of living adjustment. We would see old women dancing in the streets.

Girlfriends, we need to roll up our sleeves and work to change some of this stuff. As Harry Truman said, "The buck stops here." If we put our minds to it, we could make a lot of women's lives a lot easier. There are many opportunities to help out.

I am really serious about this. Let's help each other out. Once you have made it through some of your own money struggles, enjoy the freedom and take good care of yourself, but don't just sit back and watch other women struggling. Do something to help.

$TATI$TIC:

Working women (84%) say that quality affordable health care must be a high priority.[33]

Most single mothers are not bad citizens; they just had bad marriages. And the odds are, it will get worse for them. The numbers of deadbeat Dads, up to 2/3 of divorced fathers, are appalling, but is that the kids' fault? Society is making a much greater effort than before, but the kids are the ones who pay. Are we really going to continue to let the children suffer for the sins of these fathers?

I am not saying that single mothers are perfect, but most of them are doing their best to take care of their kids. Let's give them a break. The next time you hear a father complain about paying child support, engage him in conversation. If you are the new woman in his life, don't just agree that it is a terrible burden on him and he shouldn't pay. His children are his responsibility. They probably love him and, if your relationship with him lasts, you will be their stepmother. He may be angry with their mother, perhaps for good reason, but in trying to hurt her, he hurts his children. Guys can lose sight of this.

Now let's talk about our grandmothers and great-grandmothers. If 75% of the elderly poor are women, we all have a poor older woman in our family or our neighborhood. Figure out who she is, because she might not tell you. You might not know that she barely squeaks by each month because she's still baking those cookies for you and giving you some birthday money.

If the older woman in your family is fairly well off and generous, that's terrific. Make sure you thank her for it and tell her how much you love her. And go one step further, make an extra effort to see her. Take her to lunch or to the local museum — whatever might give her pleasure.

In every one of our neighborhoods, an elderly woman needs help. Hire your handyman for a day to work on her house, buy some food for her dog when you're at the wholesale warehouse, invite her out for lunch. If she's too proud to accept help, send her a gift anonymously — some cash in an envelope or a gift card from a nearby market. Her life will be better for it, and so will yours.

Helping others without an ulterior motive can feel great. Having a little help when things are tough can be a lifesaver. It's hard to be alone in a struggle. Bag ladies are powerful symbols because they are so alone. Perhaps that is the source of the bag lady phobia — the fear of being alone and not being able to get help. It's the financial equivalent of "I've fallen and I can't get up."

Helping old women and little kids get a little extra something, and not just at holiday time, is a true joy. Figuring out what we need and moving toward getting it is a necessity. Think about what you need — and not just those million dollars.

Get really specific about one or two things that you, or your kids, need right now to make life more manageable. Now talk about how you are going to get what you need. Brainstorm with your Moneyworks girlfriend about how are you going to make that happen. You may think about asking for a little help. Imagine that!

The Beatles song says it well: "With a Little Help From my Friends." We have the power to make this happen. It's only money.

RESOURCES:

You are the resource for my bag lady questions. I'd like to know more about this fear or phobia. Do you worry about being a bag lady or not? Why is it an issue or non-issue for you? If you have some thoughts on the bag lady syndrome, please go to my Web site at **womentalkmoney.com** and talk about it. Thanks for your help.

11. Crisis or Opportunity: Asking for Directions

You may have heard the often-quoted observation that, in Chinese, the same symbol is used to represent both crisis and opportunity. A simple symbol with a profound message: what may be a crisis may also be an opportunity.

Life's crises, we find in hindsight, were our opportunities to make changes, learn new coping strategies, and renew ourselves. Take not knowing about money or not having enough money: crisis or opportunity? In the immediate moment, it's definitely a crisis; in the long-term, we will see it was an opportunity.

Worrisome to me is that women are allowed, sometimes encouraged, to hide behind men: a father, husband, banker, trust officer, business manager. I see that as a crisis; many women see it as an opportunity. Women who leave the money management to the men in their lives feel enabled to focus on other things. I think they are disabled by not knowing about money, and I believe it will catch up with them sooner or later. Crisis or opportunity, opportunity or crisis: take your pick.

The metaphor is asking for directions. It's a running joke that men won't ask for directions when they are lost. We've all had this experience of a man refusing to ask for directions even to the point of absurdity. If we know where we're going, all is well, but if we are in unmapped — because we don't have one— territory, we're in big trouble. The woman's solution is to ask for directions; the man's is to keep driving around until he comes upon the destination.

I heard a theory that there may be a scientific basis for men's resistance to directions. Men, on the average, do not process verbal input as well as women, so that, even if they get directions, it may not help them as much as looking at a map. Intuitively, it seems like a good explanation for a long-standing and exasperating power struggle.

Think about asking for directions. When we are lost and worried, it helps to get information that points us in the right direction. We don't expect the person to get in our car and drive us to our destination. In fact, we wouldn't want them to get into our car; that is way too intrusive. Why do we let another driver take over our money?

Being dependent on men for our financial welfare is archaic at best, and downright dangerous at its worst. We all know horror stories of women, even movie stars, who have been robbed blind by the men in their lives. We know a wife who never knew about the tax returns, or the second mortgage on the home, or other debts that led to her ruin. We know a young woman who has married a man who had debts that were kept secret from her. We know a woman who has waited to inherit her father's money only to find out, at age 45 or older, that she had been removed from the will years ago. We may even *be* these women.

WI$DOM:

"I would like to see mothers staying at home to look after the children and the father taking on the traditional role of provider. It is important for the mother to always be there when the children come home from school or are ill.

Most men are usually better at understanding financial matters but women should take an interest in such things so that they are fully aware of the options open to them should they unfortunately find themselves alone."

— DAME BARBARA CARTLAND

Grief is often the crisis/opportunity that forces us to face our finances. Like the young daughter who can't imagine a time when her father won't be there to help her, none of us wants to think about losing someone that we love. We know it will happen some day, but we don't want to think about it now.

Because I didn't have a dependable — to be kind — father, I have envied women who had a father that they could count on. I have always felt that I have been on my own forever. It wasn't until very recently that I realized that it really isn't true.

In SARK's book on eating mangoes, her tribute to her father brought tears, envy, and a powerful insight into my own experience of grief. My father's disappearance was such a relief that I didn't grieve much then. My real grief came about 10 years later.

My little brother died of Hodgkin's Disease when he was 21 years old. When he died, I was 22, a new mother in an unhappy marriage. My brother and I had gotten through some really tough times together. I could count on him for anything. If ever he needed some money, I would help him, and when I needed some help, he was right there. Of course, we're talking really small sums of money because we were kids, but the safety was very important to me.

Although early grief isn't a crisis I would wish on anyone, it is a profound opportunity to value life and appreciate people while we have them. In great part, I may have become a psychologist because of grief; my own experience helps me to understand loss, particularly early loss, in others.

After my brother's death, there were two other men I knew I could count on. One, an Irish Catholic priest who didn't have a penny to his name, gave me his time and lots of it. Only in hindsight do I understand that I was catatonically depressed. This priest visited me each and every day of the week.

He understood that I couldn't talk much, but it was evident that I delighted in my beautiful little baby. The three of us sat on the floor for hours each day and played, simply. He probably saved my life, certainly my sanity. I know now that I should have been in therapy then, but that was not an option in my family, or in 1969 Baltimore. It was too great a stigma even to think about therapy, so we didn't.

The other was my father-in-law. We were as unlikely a pair as you could imagine. He was a very short, 5' 3" short, Protestant Yankee with an Ivy League education. I was a very tall, Irish Catholic, college dropout. Unlike his wife, he was proud to have me as a daughter, and he adored his grandbaby. I can still picture his grin when he presented me with the cradle that he had made for her. I knew I was safe with him too. He thought I was smart, and he insisted that I start back to school, at least part-time. Within a year, he was dead. He never got to see his second granddaughter.

$TATI$TIC:

Women, aged 25-34, earn 83 cents on the dollar compared to men. Women 55-64 earned 66 cents on the dollar.[34]

Two major losses within two years were way too much. Would my life, and my daughters' lives, have been different if my brother and my father-in-law had lived? Might I have hidden behind them? Undoubtedly so, but we don't get to pick our crises in life. We do, however, need to be prepared for them.

All of these men left me with a legacy, though not financial. My father made it very difficult for me to choose a good marriage. My brother made it possible for me to have a number of great fraternal friendships with men. My father-in-law made me respect my brain and get an education. Couldn't somebody have left me a little money?

After grief, another crisis for many women can be middle age. The words themselves sound musty. Middle age is a strange concept today. Women used to be considered middle-aged by the time they reached 35 or 40 — dried up and waiting to become old women. Tain't so today: life expectancy increases with each decade, and childbirth extends into the 40's. Middle age isn't what it used to be.

Middle age has been a different phenomenon for men and women. The culture heavily values youth in women and equates youth with beauty. It is unusual to hear anyone describe a woman over 50 as beautiful, but we believe that men get better as they age — at least Cary Grant did. I actually dated a much older guy who described himself as middle-aged at 63 — seriously. My mother said, "Does he really think he's going to live to be 126?"

Betsy Hailey talks about middle age as a "time of enormous renewal for women." It certainly has been for her. Married to playwright Oliver Hailey, Betsy had a great marriage, daughters, her books, and an endowment from her grandmother. They were having a great time, just hitting their stride, when Oliver learned he was terminally ill — the crisis we all dread.

I spoke to Betsy many months after his death. Women and money is a topic of great interest to her. Her grandmother, who had inherited money from her mother, loved keeping her own accounts. Betsy remembers her sitting on the bed, watching a baseball game, and managing her money. Her grandmother saw to it that Betsy would have some money of her own.

Oliver had grown up with very little money and was relieved that he and Betsy had some money to count on, particularly since they were both writers. Oliver loved to manage the money. He made the investment decisions and Betsy didn't mind at all. It made him happy.

As Oliver was dying, she prepared to take over the management of their money. She took her time reviewing the investments, not wanting to make decisions in the throes of her grief. And then she began to make some changes.

She put a vacation property on the market. She decided to sell their second house in England, a hard decision because the house had been very important to Oliver. It just wasn't practical for her to keep it. At that time, she made a deal for a television mini-series based on her book about her grandmother's life, *A Woman of Independent Means.* That was a breath of fresh air, and it brought in some fresh income.

Betsy discovered her own style of managing. She was beginning to replace some of their stock holdings with companies that more closely matched her social and environmental concerns. Even though they might not bring quite as high a return, the return was good enough, in her mind, to justify the shift. The decisions are hers now.

Renewal is an important phenomenon, whether for the businesswoman who chooses to have children at age 40, or the mother who has raised her children and now has time to focus on her own needs, or the single woman who is enjoying her successes and looking forward to new challenges. Middle age is a time of opportunity for women.

$TATI$TIC:

Ten million teenagers receive $1 billion a week from their parents. Amounts range from $12 to $175. Boys receive more than girls.[35]

Many stories of renewal surround us all. The 55-year-old woman starts lifting weights because of a diagnosis of osteoporosis and, within a few years, becomes a competitive weight-lifting champion in the 60+ category. The corporate woman, envied by many, leaves the boardroom to start her own company on the Web. The mom of six goes back to school and finishes her education. The battered wife is able, finally, to leave her marriage, and build a healthy life on her own. And, of course, women just like us learn to understand money, and make it work in their lives.

WI$DOM:

"I am unfit to proffer advice to today's generation of single women who are, by and large, far more sophisticated financially than I will ever be. I might, nonetheless, suggest the following to any wife who remains as fiscally naïve as I one was: learn every detail of your husband's business world, and prepare to assume control in case of emergency.

A word of explanation: I spent 20 wonderful years as a bird in a gilded cage. My masterful husband handled everything — houses, investments, careers, the world. Meanwhile I practiced a form of shoplifting. Innocent of a checking account or credit card, I wandered through boutiques, picking up desired articles and wafting them away, while clerks followed me about, taking notes and charging the lot to Bing Crosby. Not a bad life, you might remark, and there was a time when I'd have agreed wholeheartedly, but that was before the loadstone of that paradise disappeared, and I found myself in the hands of rapacious lawyers, determined to loot an estate that I hadn't known existed. Fortunately, Bing, provident to the last, had left me his most trusted friend to fend them off and educate me. Otherwise I would have suffered the fate of numerous acquaintances who, with their husbands, lost all their worldly goods."

— KATHRYN CROSBY

Possibly the toughest crisis in the life of a happily married woman is when her husband dies suddenly or when he is diagnosed with his final illness. If he's been driving, so to speak, for many years, she can be left trying to thumb a ride. I have not heard a more painful cry from an adult than a new widow sobbing, "What am I going to do?"

If the husband's death is sudden, she is thrown into making major financial decisions while she can barely see straight because of grief and shock. She is alone, perhaps for the first time in her life. Imagine what that would be like for the woman who has never written a check.

I have always supposed that with the knowledge that there is a year or so left in a life, the couple has time to plan and put things in order, so they will be prepared. However, I spoke to a woman who specializes in working with older couples and she says the contrary. The couples are often plunged into depression about his illness, so they don't talk about practical matters at all. They can't face it together, so she faces it alone.

If we can hear about these crises and try to create an opportunity to learn from them, it will make our grief processes a bit more bearable. Remember, if your partner dies, you have to make immediate decisions about the funeral or memorial arrangements; these alone can be very costly. We need to know about stuff way ahead of time, before the crisis finds us.

Time and time again, women tell me that we have to know where everything is. That includes any or all of the following: checkbooks, savings passbooks, bank cards, credit cards, tax returns, life insurance policies, disability insurance policies, health insurance cards and policies, stock portfolios, bonds, the deed for the house and other properties, credit reports, keys to safe deposit boxes, and wills. In today's electronic world, we also need to know the passwords to any online accounts and the pin numbers for any automatic teller or credit cards. See how much there can be to track down?

I hear horror stories all the time about women who don't have the first idea where the money is, or, even, the name of the accountant. If you have a partner who doesn't want you to know these things, look out. The benign interpretation is a misguided sense of protectiveness; ask to not be protected quite so thoroughly. The malignant interpretation is that your partner is hiding something or has an extreme need to control you; that's a much more difficult problem.

For couples who have larger holdings, there will probably be some kind of family trust, but you need input on that too. For some couples, there may not be any assets; you still need to know about all of the debt and any life insurance. Even a small life insurance policy provided by the employer could help a lot in a crisis.

$TATI$TIC:

Only 48% of African American women and 33% of Latinas have retirement savings vs. 71% of white women and 68% of Asian Americans.[36]

If you have elderly parents, and if they will give out the information, it will be helpful to know where all of their stuff is. And for single moms or couples with young children, it is essential that someone is appointed to be in charge in the unlikely, but horrible, event that something happens. Even a short-term hospitalization because of an accident can leave children stranded.

If I could pick only one or two items to know about in the event of a death, it would be the life insurance policy and the ATM cards. Life insurance can be a lifesaver in a time of need. Any reputable life insurance company will pay the beneficiary very quickly once they receive the death certificate. This money has gotten many a widow through tough times. Of course, the ATM cards provide ready access to cash in the account, 24 hours a day.

In the 1970's, my friend Buz's husband died suddenly, and while they were separated. A CEO of a Fortune 500 company, he had a severe problem with alcohol and, after 30 years of marriage, she had asked him to leave. He moved into his mother's house and, literally, drank himself to death. The mother-in-law did not even inform Buz of his death; a friend called to offer condolences. Buz quickly dressed the two younger children still at home and called the others to get to the church for the funeral.

In the midst of her shock and grief, she learned that he had cut off all of her accounts, and changed his will leaving nothing to her or the older children. She had been the quintessential corporate wife and, all of a sudden, she was destitute in a big house on Long Island. If she hadn't had an insurance policy on his life, she doesn't know what she would have done. That check came within a few days and she needed every penny of it to support herself and to pay for the years of litigation over the estate. Even though it was a grueling and heart-wrenching battle, her story had a happy ending. Many widows' stories do not.

Most crises in life surprise us; we have no option but to scramble to handle them. If we can predict some crises, so that the opportunities are readily accessible, let's do it. Let's try to embrace our opportunities.

Let's take this opportunity to go shopping. You and your Money works girlfriend need to shop for a large, loose-leaf binder to store your records. Don't think about all the papers or information you will need to find right now. Now, it's just time to shop. Go to your local stationery store or a large office supply warehouse, whichever would be more fun for you.

Pick out a large 3-hole binder, 3 inches or so wide. They come in many colors and styles nowadays — choose a color that feels like hope and success to you. Also, buy some dividers with tabs, maybe a dozen or so. You might want to pick dividers that have a built-in pocket where you can put bankbooks or credit cards. If you don't have a 3-hole punch at home, buy one of those too. It's a shopping spree.

WI$DOM:

"Don't look at catalogs on a day you need a 'pick-me-up.' My mother-in-las has said for 18 years, "Honey, tuck something away in your bra each month. He doesn't have to know." Well, this little lady has saved more in her bra than I have ever been able to put away in a savings account. I better start wearing fuller woman-size bras soon."

— KATHY LENNON DARIS

You don't have to do it right now, but when you are ready, the binder will be your steady companion. Eventually, it will contain all of your financial records in case of an emergency. For the moment, let's just make the first two sections.

Start with Section 1, the life insurance policies. After you find the policy, insert it behind the first divider. Label the tab, "Life Insurance." If there are two or more policies, do the same with them. You may want to make a list of them and put it in the front of this section with any contact persons, phone numbers, or addresses.

Section 2 is for ready cash bank cards and pin numbers. You

can organize the statements for each card or make a list. You'll figure out your own priority for the rest of the sections later. They will include any or all of the items listed a few pages ago.

Once you have gathered all your financial information in one place, then you have a clearer picture of what's going on. That doesn't mean that you'll be asking for a crisis, but it does mean that you'll be more ready for one when it happens. Remember: it's only money.

RESOURCES:

In any crisis, we need people we can count on. Chances are that you already know who will be there for you emotionally in a crisis. Think about someone else who can help with the financial details and decision-making in the short run, because you will need help. It may be your best friend, a sibling, or an adult child. It may be your insurance agent, accountant, broker, banker, or trust officer. These working relationships that you have developed over time can be unbelievably helpful in a crisis. It is essential that you know you can trust their judgment while you are in distress.

12. Don't Touch My God-forbid Money

Tina, the sister of my friend Ron, is terrific with money. Tina doesn't make a ton of money as a school secretary, but she knows the magic of budgeting. She has remodeled her house – one room at a time — by negotiating good bargains with workmen and local stores. She takes a nice vacation almost every year, and she never spends money she doesn't have.

For Tina, the single most important element in her money magic is saving — having a cushion put away in case of an emergency. Tina calls it her "God-forbid Money." That cushion makes her feel safe. Tina says, "You don't really need those six new pairs of shoes if you don't have a cushion. You know what's really important? The God-forbid money: that's what is really important."

Budgeting, saving, investing are some of the very words that turn us away from traditional money management books. When our money is unknown or out of control, these sensible words sound alien to us, but are they?

Women are investing all the time. We invest in our friends. We invest in our families. We invest in our colleagues at work. We get to know these people. We make decisions about how much or how little to invest in these relationships. We nurture them, watch them grow, and count on these people for support when we need it. We feel secure to know that we have them; they are our emotional cushions.

$TATI$TIC:

In 1972, 4.6% of US businesses were owned by women.[37] By 1997, 1/3 of all US businesses were women-owned.[38]

Occasionally, a friendship or other relationship doesn't work out. Sad as it may be, we try to cut our losses and extricate ourselves from it. When that happens, we analyze the situation to understand what went wrong, and we apply the information to future relationships.

Investing our money requires the same skills that we use to build our relationships, but the idea of investing makes us very anxious. Perhaps we need to think of it as shopping. Most of us love to get a good buy: high-quality goods at the best possible prices.

With investing, we get an additional bonus. We can get a lot of use out of an investment, but if we decide after a few months or years that we don't want it anymore, we can exchange it. We can even make money on the deal.

Let's define investing very broadly for the moment. Any time we make a decision about where to put our money, it could be considered investing. Even how we spend our money, and how much of it we spend – in other words, budgeting — is a type of investing. We all have to make decisions about which brand of coffee to buy, which credit card to accept, which savings account best suits our needs, which mortgage to take, and so on.

We've actually been investing without realizing it. The next step is to determine if our investment decisions have been wise, which investments to keep and which to change. Now we have some concrete work to do.

We can start by looking at the bank or credit union where we keep our checking accounts. One careful look at the monthly statement will tell us what the monthly fee is for that account. It may be 0 or it may be $12 or more a month. At an average figure of $8, we are spending $96 a year for the privilege of writing checks from that bank. Is that okay or would you rather have a $96 cushion put away? At a basic level, asking that question is a form of investing.

$TATI$TIC:

In 1998, 79% of men ages 65-74 were married vs. 55 % of women. At 85 or older, 50% of men were married vs. 13% of women.[39]

Pick up a few brochures from local banks. Examine the other charges like ATM fees, printing costs, customer service fees, etc. Maybe it's time to try a different bank or a different type of account in that bank. If you have access to a credit union, often those are the most economical, but may not be as convenient because they have fewer locations than a major bank.

Here's another tip: when you think about how much something costs you, think in terms of a year, not a month. That's what good money managers do. Something that might cost you $20 a month might not sound like such a good deal at $240 a year.

You may be amazed at how much money you can save in a year by shopping for a better checking account. And, if you are a student or a senior, defined as 55 years of age at some banks, you may qualify for a free account with free checks. You may even be able to earn interest on the money in your checking account. Imagine that! Managing our money is that simple.

Let's talk a bit about saving. Many women have told me how important it is to save money. That may seem impossible to you – that you just don't make enough money to put some away – and sometimes it's true. But think about it again. Is it really impossible, or do we think saving has to mean large sums of money like 10% or 20% of our income? Even if we save only 25 cents a day, we are still saving, and it gives us a start toward having a little cushion.

I know a high-powered agent in Hollywood who makes a great deal of money by most standards. Every year, her accountant

tells her that she has to put some money in the bank, and, every year, she gets angry with him. She says that, as a single mother with a little boy, it takes every penny she makes to pay for living in Los Angeles. Maybe she's setting the bar too high. She probably can save $2 a week; that's less than 1/10th of one per cent of her income. Such a small goal may seem ridiculous to her, but it is better than nothing.

A small goal is usually attainable; then, we can go for the bigger goals. After we save $50, we can work on another $50. Once we have $100, we can work toward another $100.

WI$DOM:

"When you're older, having your own home — paid for — is important. Try to enjoy life. If all else fails, get a cat." — NOEL NEILL

Recently, I had a conversation with an extremely successful businessman who talked about saving. He had taken a job with a company that had a history of firing executives within two years. Knowing that, he decided to save three months' worth of money so, if he got fired, he would have a cushion because an executive job search may take many months. He talked quite honestly about just how hard it was to save that much money, but he had set his goal and stuck to the plan.

As he put it, "The first $35,000 was the hardest; then it got easier." After he saved three months' worth of money, it grew to six months' worth. Not only did the company not fire him, he had a once-in-a-lifetime opportunity to buy into the company during hard times. He said the same thing that successful women have told me, "Without that cash in the bank, it wouldn't have been possible." He would have missed out.

I am not expecting you to save $35,000 in a short period of time, but I do want you to set a goal that makes sense for your circumstances. It may be $15 or $50 or $500 or $5,000. You are the only one who can decide on this first amount. Pick a number that is within your reach, so that you have a high probability of success. When you achieve that goal, set another one, and keep on going.

If you had been fortunate enough to get off to a good start with money, that is what your parents would have taught you. Small, short-term goals lead to both quick and long-term rewards. You will be investing in your own success.

If you have dependents, think about buying life insurance. By dependents, I mean a spouse, children, and/or an elderly parent who need your financial support. There are several different kinds of insurance: whole life, term, etc. Premiums are more or less expensive based on whether or not the policies have any cash value. Suffice it to say that it is possible to pay a very small premium to provide at least some protection for your family.

Insurance agents make their living by helping people pick the right policy for their needs. They make a commission from the companies; you don't have to pay a fee for their advice. Be careful to stick to your budget (oops, that word again). You can always buy more, or different, insurance later when there is more money for it.

Let's talk about investing as we traditionally think of it: buying stocks and bonds. More and more women are buying into the stock market. Remember the shopping analogy: buy high-quality goods at a good price. Buying stocks and bonds takes the same skills you use in the stores: assessing the value and cost. That's all investing is: shopping with some high-falutin' terms attached to it.

Unless you are a genius, or perfect, you must know that you are going to make some mistakes. Mistakes are opportunities for us to learn. You may choose a stock that loses money, or you may wish you had bought more of a stock that makes a lot of money. Give yourself a little time to learn.

My friend J is a seasoned investor, but she wasn't always. When she was learning, she sometimes made money and sometimes lost money. Not much of a gambler, she likes to minimize her risk. Nowadays, she does a fair amount of research – asking a lot of questions and reading – before she makes an investment.

$TATI$TIC:

Women's investment clubs earned 21.3% annual return compared to 15% for men-only clubs.[40]

Let's talk about taking risks for a minute. Every woman I know has taken some risks in her life. Not every single risk pays off, of course, but I can guarantee you that not taking any risks will keep things pretty much as they are. If your *status quo* is great, that's just fine, but I don't think you are reading this book because your *status quo* is terrific.

I am going to make the assumption that you want to make some changes. Since you've gotten this far, you probably have started making some changes already.

Risk is an individual phenomenon; you need to know how much risk you can tolerate. There is not a generic right or wrong answer to the question of risk-taking. Some women are skydivers and others like to keep their feet on the ground. Some women are very cautious and need to feel safe most of the time. Others are willing to take a big chance for a big payoff. Still others want to take some chances, but with fairly good odds that they will benefit.

A friend of Betsy Hailey's told me a funny story about her first investment risk. Veronica was working as a typist on the Smothers Brothers' television show. She felt really lucky to have landed a job in TV. One of the cameramen gave her a hot stock tip. I don't know why, but they are always called hot stock tips — maybe because we get burned. Veronica took every penny she had saved and bought shares in this mining company. She was thrilled: a job in TV, and any minute she was going to be rich.

Within a few weeks, the company had gone bust; she lost her entire investment. Veronica had taken a big risk on what she thought was a sure thing, but she learned her lesson. She began to ask questions and read; she started to invest wisely. Today, she reads the Wall Street *Journal* each morning, tracking her stocks and the fluctuations in the international money market. She still keeps that stock certificate from her first investment as a reminder of what not to do.

Risk and benefit are two very important concepts. If we balance the risks and benefits of any situation with our own tolerance level, we have the formula to make solid decisions, financial and otherwise. Know your tolerance level and pay attention to it.

If you would like to buy some stock, or you want to begin learning about a stock portfolio that you already own, sit down with your Moneyworks girlfriend and talk about it. Start reading and asking questions about a particular company that interests you. You may want to learn about the company's history, products, leadership, future plans, the high and low prices of the stock in the past 3-5 years, and anything else that interests you. Companies will gladly send you their annual reports. In most cases, you can buy only one share if you don't have a lot of money to invest right now.

There's a great old (1956) black and white movie called *The*

Solid Gold Cadillac. Judy Holliday plays a small investor who goes to a stockholders' meeting and starts asking a lot of questions. A very funny comedy, she takes on a crooked Board of Directors and saves the day. Look for it on late-night television. It's a great lesson in investing.

If you aren't ready to enter the stock market right now, don't worry about it. Focus on saving and getting rid of any credit card debt you may have. Keep the stock market in mind for the future.

WI$DOM:

"Respect it. Educate yourself about economics." — MARLA GIBBS

The interest you save by beginning to pay off the credit cards may be the best investment you can make right now. If you are paying 15-20% interest on a balance of $1,000, you are paying out $150-200 per year in interest. Most stocks will not give you that high a return, and no bank will pay that much on a savings account.

Let's talk about inheritance. Talk about emotional trap! Try to not invest too much energy in your inheritance. I have seen far too many women invest a lot of time, and service, because of money they hope to get some day. In many cases, if we are only doing it for the money, it's a poor investment.

A lot can happen in 10 or 20 or 50 years. Marriages can end, wills can be changed, aging fathers can remarry and have a new set of children, or a rich family can be ruined by medical costs. Waiting for an inheritance can be a life sentence.

The mother of one of my dearest friends left her a large sum of money when she died. She was amazed that her mother had put so much money away over the years and, also, relieved that she could stop worrying about her retirement account. Then she learned that her father, a very controlling man, found a loophole to prevent her from receiving her mother's endowment.

$TATI$TIC:

In 2000, 35% of recent college graduates with student loan debt also had other debt payments of $1,000 per month, up from 10% in 1991.[41]

My friend thought, as did I, that her father would relent and comply with her mother's wishes, but he didn't. She even met with him and his lawyer to try to resolve the conflict, but to no avail. Her mother's money has been put into a trust for my friend's adult children. She will never see a penny of it herself, and her children cannot have it until after she dies. She will remain, her father thinks, under his control — precisely what her mother tried to prevent.

Machiavellian as this story is, there are many others like it. People with a strong need to control who use their resources, including money, as weapons. Thank goodness, my friend is a capable woman who has not counted on an inheritance to support her.

An income of our own, freedom from heavy debts, and growing investments will ensure our financial independence and security. Having enough money can be a dream come true.

Think about that "God-forbid money." How big a cushion would help you to feel safer? Talk to your Moneyworks friend about what you could do right now to begin to create that cushion for yourself. You might put pennies into a piggybank or dollars into a savings account, or transfer a large sum from checking to savings.

Having a cushion is like tying a pillow around you when you first learn to skate. If you do fall down, you will have some protection. The bigger the cushion, the more protection we have when we need it.

RESOURCES:

Your bank statements and credit card bills contain information about interest rates, service charges, and other fees. Brochures from banks and brokerage houses list the services, options, and costs. You might need a magnifying glass for some of the fine print.

When you are ready to invest in stocks, the experiences of the Beardstown Ladies will teach you a lot about making solid investments. They are a group of older women who started an investment club and have done very well. They have written a couple of very readable books.

You may want to visit the Women's Financial Network (wfn.com) at Seibert and Company on the Web. Founded by women for women, it's a good place to start.

13. We Can Do It, We Can Do It

P icture those little Disney mice singing while they sew a new dress for "Cinderelly." The ugly stepsisters have given her so many chores that Cinderella doesn't have time to fix her dress for the Ball. Enlisting the help of the birds, the little mice take on this big job, singing in high-pitched voices. And they do it.

When money starts getting you down or you feel over-whelmed, think about those little mice. If we work together, we can do it too. By next week or next month or next year, we can be in much better shape financially.

If a computer were to analyze the content of my many conversations about money with women, several concepts would stand out clearly. Save, save, save. Budget and plan. Ask questions about what you don't know. Set goals. Get rid of credit card debt.

Teach your children about money. Take risks, but know what they are. And, thank goodness, have fun.

I have talked to women from all over this country and found that women from very diverse backgrounds echo each other's words. There must be something to it.

We know that we need to have enough money. We know that enough money is a relative concept that will be different for each of us. We know that we need to have a cushion, but the amount of that cushion can vary from $100 up to $200,000, or more, depending on each woman's situation. That is one clear objective we can all set today: to have a cushion.

We know that the earlier we start learning about money, the better it will be for us. We must remember that for our kids' sake. However, many financially comfortable women didn't begin to think about money until they were well into adulthood. It is, literally, never too late to begin dealing with money more constructively.

Let's think about it in terms of the life span. The average life expectancy goes up each year and, on the average, women live longer than men. We know that women make less money than men and most women do not accrue as much in pensions or Social Security benefits as men. Therefore, in all probability, we are going to live more years than men do, and on less money.

The older celebrity women in this book advise us to save money. Joan Fontaine said, "SAVE IT!" Dina Merrill said, "Save for a rainy day." These are two extremely successful and famous women who are clearly concerned about the need to save. Fannie Flagg, comedienne and novelist, advises that we "Start a pension plan — at an early age."

If you are a young woman reading this book, I hope you will take their advice to heart. What you do now may have a powerful effect on your older years. I know it's hard to think about that now, but now is the time to build the base for your financial future.

If you are in high school or just graduating, open a checking account of your own. Try to get one with no monthly service charges. Start building your relationship with your local bank now. Trisha Yearwood's father made sure she had a checkbook in high school and he taught her how to balance it. She said, "Know your own business and take responsibility for where your money is invested and how it is spent."

It is never too early to save. If you put only $1 a week into a savings account, you will have approximately $8,000 in 50 years when you may really need it. The actual amount you contributed in those 50 years is only $2600 but, even at a conservative interest rate of 4% per year, the miracle of compound interest turns that $2600 into $8,000. If you could save $10 a week, you will have $80,000 in the same time period. The fewer years you save, the less the money will be worth.

Even a young woman can have her own investment account. You can buy individual stocks or invest in a mutual fund. You may do as Nora Ephron's mother did, pick a product or a company that you like (hers was Tampax). Read up on the company in investment magazines or newspapers, for example, *Investors' Business Daily* or the *Wall Street Journal*. You might talk to a stockbroker, a family member, or a teacher about it, but make your own decision.

Once you've decided which stock or fund you want, you can

buy it through a broker in person or on the internet through one of the online trading companies. The fee is usually less if you buy online. The same is true about buying shares of a mutual fund, and many funds don't charge a fee. Pick a family of funds, then select the one specific fund that best matches your needs. Again, you can read all about it in magazines or business newspapers. Talk about it, read, and make a plan.

You'll be making decisions about a career path in the next few years. Investigate the areas expected to be most in need in the next 10-20 years. Think widely about what your talents are, and how you might best use them to succeed in the job market.

Be careful to include job areas that may be male-dominated also. Those might be the jobs that pay the best salary. When you are offered your first job, ask for a little more money. It doesn't hurt to ask and, who knows, you might just get it.

If you are in college right now, unless your parents are paying all your costs, you may be particularly vulnerable to debt that can last you a lifetime. Student loans are a blessing in that you may not be able to go to college without them, but see if there are any other ways to pay for your education.

Loans sound so simple: the school helps you get them, the check arrives at the beginning of each semester, and your tuition is paid. You don't begin paying them back until you graduate, and you have 20 years to pay them off. Easy, right?

Talk to recent graduates and ask questions about their loan payments. In the 21st century, a private college will cost over $100,000 for four years. That can mean that you will have payments of $700 or more per month until you are 45 years old. Look for other ways to finance school -- an extra job, grants, and contributions from other relatives. Perhaps you may choose a less expensive school or a public university. Talk about it, read, and make a plan.

Credit card companies target college students. They offer student credit cards with low interest rates that may seem very appealing. If you listen to the stories of women who began to accumulate their credit card debt in college, you'll think twice about these seductive offers.

While it may be necessary to have a credit card in your name, it is also important to pay the balance off each month. Don't be seduced into spending money you don't have. Your financial history begins at a young age, so must financial learning. Talk about it, read, and make a plan.

If you are a young single woman just out of high school or college and working in your first job, you have a great opportunity to begin building for your future. It is time to work hard, set your goals, and be determined to work toward those goals. It is also time to enjoy your money and have fun.

If you have no debt, that's great. You can begin building your assets by saving and investing. If your company has a pension or 401k plan, get involved in it. Think about an individual retirement account for yourself, a Roth IRA or an IRA; a little money put away now grows enormously over the years. Perhaps you will want to buy property -- a condominium or a house -- to live in. You are in

a perfect position to construct a solid base for yourself. Talk about it, read, and make a plan.

For young single women who have accumulated debt, your first priority may be to get out of debt. I know how hard it can be to look at debt, but looking at it is the first step to getting out from under. Try this: make a list of every debt you have and the interest rate on those debts. If you can stand it, try one more thing: sort the list starting with the account with the highest rate first down to the one with lowest interest rate. Keep that list.

If you are fortunate, you may get some help paying off this debt. You may have options like a loan from your family or a consolidation loan from a bank. However, if you have to pay it all back a little at a time, there's a trick to it. Look at your list. Always pay a little extra, even $5, each month to the account with the highest interest rate until it is paid off. Talk about it, read, and make a plan.

If you are a single woman considering joining your life with another person, discuss your values with each other. Talk about money, children, property, investments, debt, and how you see the future. You also need to know each other's financial situation: assets, liabilities, credit history, and goals for the future. Talking now will prevent a lot of stress in the years to come.

As Christine Baranski says, "Marry for love – never for financial security." The more you and your prospective mate love each other and share similar values, the better off you will be. Remember that this may be a life-long contract that ties all of your behavior together – past, present, and future.

If you are a married woman, you must know about the financial circumstances of your marriage, with or without children. Dame Barbara Cartland wrote from England to advocate the traditional roles of mother and provider, but also emphasized that women must be "fully aware of the options open to them." Kathryn Crosby wrote a plea to wives about the down-side of being the often-envied "bird in a gilded cage."

Too many women leave too much of the financial burden and the financial power in their husbands' hands, thinking that it is his responsibility to earn, invest, and plan for the future. Marriage is a partnership and you are equally responsible for your family's finan-cial state. Your husband may be around longer if you share the financial stress with him. Talk about it, and make a plan together.

You may want to keep a separate account in addition to your joint accounts. Linda Ellerbee says, "Keep your money. Fall in love. But keep your money." Pay special attention to the advice of for-mer Senator Carol Moseley-Braun; heed her suggestions about spending and planning for retirement. Talk about it, read, and make a plan.

For all women, single or in relation-ships, who have the resources, you can hire financial advisors to assist you with your money as both Julia Child and Ivana Trump suggest. Remember that the key word is "assist." Pay attention to your money. Know where it is invested and why. It is impor-tant to know what your advisors are doing and whether you agree with their decisions. Talk about it, read, and make a plan.

If you are a mother, understand that your children are learning about money from you. What you know and how you behave will determine their behavior to some extent. Teach your children well. They need to know about value, saving for what they want, spending wisely, and planning. Start them with saving accounts when they are little and a checking account in high school or college. Give them some sort of allowance no matter how small and help them learn how to manage it. They need to know about interest, both the kind you earn and the kind you pay.

As one young man said to his bride, "We want to be the people who earn interest, not the people who pay interest." Teach your children to talk about it, read, and make a plan.

If you have children who are college students, ask them about their credit card debt. See if you can help them to understand the implications of having sizeable debt. If you are able and willing, consider giving them a loan to clear these high-interest debts.

If you are faced with divorce, look carefully at your assets including pensions, IRAs, and stock options. The settlement that you negotiate will affect you and your children for years to come. Carolyn See insists that you "take the house" if it is offered to you.

If you have small children, try to negotiate a contract about their school expenses and, particularly, college costs. Remember that child support payments end at age 18. College costs are soaring and courts cannot force parents to pay those costs. Think also about your own retirement needs and your earning power. Divorce is very stressful, but get the best advice you can. Talk about it, read, and make a plan.

If you have been a single mother, you may have been so busy supporting your children that you have reached middle age with very little thought, or money, dedicated to your own future. Don't despair. Now is the time that you will begin to focus on your own goals. You may be getting a late start, but starting now is better than not starting at all. Make an assessment of your financial state: income, assets, and any retirement dollars you may have accumulated. Talk about it, read, and make a plan.

If you are to be a widow, you will be much better off if you know the financial facts and have developed skills for handling the money on your own. Sadly, statistics tell us that the husband will probably die before his wife. Of course, this does not happen in all cases, but, the more skilled you are financially, the more energy you will have for recovering from the trauma of losing your lifetime partner. Now is the time to talk about it, read, and make a plan.

If you are an older woman, you may find that life can open up in unexpected ways. If you are healthy, there is much to explore, like lifting weights, taking classes, trying a new job, and learning about money. If you are struggling financially, there may be some ways to increase income and reduce expenses. If you have a house, that may be a source of income for you. If you are comfortable financially but don't know much about your investments — <u>yet</u> — now is the time to learn. It's your money. You may want to think about an investment club or design a family trust. Talk about it, read, and make a plan.

If you have a moderate or sizeable estate, think seriously about a fair plan for distributing your money, both now and after your death. Consider giving to two or three generations, not just to your children; shake up the power dynamics a little. The law, at this point, allows gifts of up to $10,000 per year with no tax penalties. Maybe you'll want to do that.

Keep in mind that 50-50 isn't always equal. You may want to bequeath different amounts to different children and grandchildren, depending on their circumstances. Remember that 30% disparity. If you decide to do this, try to talk to your family about it, so there will be no surprises. Money and grief often mix in a really unpleasant way.

For all of us, there is so much more to learn about money if we set our minds to it. Across the life span, women learn new information, whether it's about taking a photograph, exercising, or having money. Anxiety can be a major block to new learning, but anxiety is manageable. Not dealing with our anxiety only makes it worse. Learn to breathe through the anxiety. We need to keep trying new things until money doesn't scare us anymore. It's only money.

If an expert is talking "over your head" about money, stop listening to him or her, but don't stop listening to everyone. Find someone who talks at a level you can understand. If you pick up a book about money that is too complicated for you, then put that book down. Look for a book that meets your needs. Magazine articles may be a good place to start.

There are many good books about money management on the market today. Some of them are written for women by women. Some are written in general by women and by men. Your job is to find the books that speak to you. One of my favorites is

YES YOU CAN Achieve Financial Independence by James E. Stowers, but it may not be the book for you. There are "niche" books for unique groups, e.g., divorced women, single mothers, and widows. Cheryl Broussard's book, *The Black Woman's Guide to Financial Independence*, is an excellent example.

If you have started to talk about money, you are well on your way to having enough money. You're ready to go on to other sources: financial magazines or newspapers, and books about money management. We can do this. Just talk about it, read, make plans, and enjoy life. As Charles Dickens said, "Result happiness." And always remember that it's only money.

Acknowledgments

I am deeply grateful to the many men and women who stood by me as this book took shape. First and foremost, my agent nonpareil, Edward Hibbert, has been steadfast, energetic, and smashingly funny even in the difficult times. I don't think I could have done this without him; I know I wouldn't have had as good a time. Warm thanks also to Jesse Dorris, Neal Olson, and Ira Silverberg at Donadio & Olson for their faith in me.

Many, many thanks to the women who lent me their stories and their thoughts about women and money: Phoebe Beasley, Cheryl Broussard, Carol Carter, Veronica Chambers, Billie Elias, Elizabeth Forsythe Hailey, Pearl Miller, Saralie, Carolyn See, Tina Silverman, Buz Walters, and Dr. Joycelyn Whiten. Also to the women who preferred not to be identified by name, I thank you for your great stories.

For their wise, poignant, and witty words, I appreciate the

generosity of Robyn Astaire, Christine Baranski, Nell Carter, Dame Barbara Cartland, Julia Child, Kathryn Crosby, Tyne Daly, Kathy Lennon Daris, Blossom Dearie, Ruby Dee, Olympia Dukakis, Dr. Joycelyn Elders, Linda Ellerbee, Nora Ephron, Fannie Flagg, Joan Fontaine, Marla Gibbs, Dina Merrill, Former Senator Carol Moseley-Braun, Noel Neill, Ivana Trump, and Trisha Yearwood for responding to my request for advice.

Having so many friends to thank makes me realize how rich my life is. Singling out a few for their "above and beyond" is necessary. Otts Munderloh, my "oldest" friend and soundman extraordinaire, was at the ready with audio equipment and computer hardware and software to make my life easier; his unwavering, unconditional support was immeasurable. Dick Scanlan was the first to read the initial proposal; he gave me a hard push to speak my mind. My "backers," Susan Wadsworth and Michael Marquart, provided many a great dinner and immense support throughout. Fred E. Basten lent his many years of experience and a friendly ear whenever I needed it. Rose B. Germaine made me make the Web site happen and kept me on track all the way. Paul Guido, Steve Blain, Scott Sherman, and Ron Celona provided beautiful settings where I could get over even the toughest writing blocks, and they suggested a few interviewees as well. Tony Battaglia and Merry Lee were my cheerleaders, and they bought the balloons. Clara Farah and Dottie Brewer have been great coaches. Maryellen and Maureen have made me laugh forever. I am grateful to these and many more. You have all been terrific.

`And last, but never least, my ever-growing family constantly amazes me. My mother, Liz Roberson, is my best sales rep. My daughters, their husbands, and their beautiful little girls bring joy to my life by their very existence.

Los Angeles, California
April 2002

APPENDIX A

"THE PENSION 8" (FROM PAGE 77):

1. Find out if you are earning or have ever earned a pension.

2. If your employer has a pension plan, find out how you can be eligible.

3. Contribute to a pension plan if you have the chance.

4. If you leave your job, do not spend your pension if you are given a one-time payment.

5. If you are married, find out if your husband has a pension.

6. Do not sign away a future right to your husband's pension if you become widowed.

7. During divorce, consider the pension as a valuable, jointly earned asset to be divided.

8. Find out about your pension rights and fight for them.

Statistical References

1. Crossette, Barbara, "UN Documents Inequities for Women as World Forum Nears," *New York Times*, 18 August 1995, National edition, Sec. A, pg. 3.

2. Mead, Walter, "Domestic Saints in the Next Revolution," *Worth*, April 1994, pg. 41-43.

3. Avins, Mimi, "Closing the Financial Literacy Gap," *Los Angeles Times*, 9 May 2000, Sec. E, pg. 1.

4. "Those Who Get Welfare Do Not Fit Stereotypes," *Investors Business Daily*, 17 September 1996, pg. 1.

5. Cohen, Patricia, "Oops, Sorry: Seems That My Pie Chart is Half-baked," *New York Times*, 8 April 2000, National edition, Arts and Ideas Section, pg. 15.

6, Kilborn, Peter T., "More Women Take Low-Wage Jobs Just So Their Families Can Get By," *New York Times*, 13 March 1994, National edition, pg. 11.

7. Mead, Walter, "Domestic Saints in the Next Revolution," *Worth*, April 1994, pg. 41-43.

8. Kilborn, Peter T., "More Women Take Low-Wage Jobs Just So Their Families Can Get By," *New York Times*, 13 March 1994, National edition, pg. 11.

9. "Married Women Spur 150% Hike in Family Income, *Credentials Newsletter*, Vol. XII Issue 1, July 1999, pg. 1.

10. Editorial, "No Hidden Agenda, Just Improving Women's Lives," *USA Today*, 24 August 1995, pg. 16A.

11. Kilborn, Peter T. "Women and Minorities Still Face 'Glass Ceiling'," *New York Times*, 16 March 1995, National edition, pg. C22.

12. Mead, Walter, "Domestic Saints in the Next Revolution," *Worth*, April 1994, pg. 41-43.

13. Roberts, Sam, "Women's Work: What's New, What Isn't," *New York Times*, National edition, pg. A12.

14. Mead, Walter, "Domestic Saints in the Next Revolution," *Worth*, April 1994, pg. 41-43.

15. *ibid.*

16. "Single Women and Poverty: Study Shows a Strong Link," *New York Times*, 19 February 1994, National edition, pg. 14.

17. Lewin, Tamar, "Union Links Women's Pay to Poverty Among Families," *New York Times*, 25 February 1999, National edition, pg. A17.

18. Schembari, James, "New College Sticker Shock: Junior's Credit Card Bill," *New York Times*, 27 February 2000, National edition, Business section, pg. 12.

19. Nicholson, Trish, "Women and Investing: Getting in the Swim," *AARP Bulletin*, April 2000, pg. 14.

20. Wolf, Naomi, "Women, Money, and Power," *Los Angeles Times*, 6 February 1994, Book Review section, pg. 4.

21. Schembari, James, "New College Sticker Shock: Junior's Credit Card Bill," *New York Times*, 27 February 2000, National edition, Business section, pg. 12.

22. Avins, Mimi, "Closing the Financial Literacy Gap," *Los Angeles Times*, 9 May 2000, Sec. E, pg. 1.

23. Harney, Kenneth R., "U.S. Probes Higher Fees for Women, Minorities," *Los Angeles Times*, 24 September 1995, pg. K4.

24. Lewin, Tamar, "Working Women Say Bias Persists," *New York Times*, 15 October 1994, National edition, pg. 8.

25. Noble, Barbara Presley, "Unhealthy Prospects for Women," *New York Times*, 22 May 1994, National edition, pg. 23.

26. Mead, Walter, "Domestic Saints in the Next Revolution," *Worth*, April 1994, pg. 41-43.

27. "1 in 4 Work in Women-Owned Firms In US," *Los Angeles Times*, 27 March 1997, Section D, pg. 2.

28. Lewin, Tamar, "Income Gap Between Sexes Found to Widen in Retirement," *New York Times*, 26 April 1995, National edition, pg. A15.

29. Jaffe, Charles, "A Lesson Plan for Teaching Kids How to Handle Money," *Los Angeles Times*, 12 October 1996, pg. D1.

30. Kilborn, Peter T., "More Women Take Low-Wage Jobs Just So Their Families Can Get By," *New York Times*, 13 March 1994, National edition, pg. 11.

31. Roberts, Sam, "Women's Work: What's New, What Isn't," *New York Times*, National edition, pg. A12.

32. "Head Count," *My Generation*, March-April 2001, pg. 26.

33. Greenhouse, Steven, "Poll of Working Women Finds Them Stressed," *New York Times*, 10 March 2000, National edition, pg. A13.

34. Lewin, Tamar, "Study Says More Women Earn Half Their Household Income," *New York Times*, 26 April 1995, National edition, pg. A13.

35. Wells, Susan J., "The Affluence of Youth, Thanks to Mom and Dad," *New York Times*, 5 March 2000, National edition, Business section, pg. 12.

36. Nicholson, Trish, "Women and Investing: Getting in the Swim," *AARP Bulletin*, April 2000, pg. 14.

37. Card, Emily and Adam Miller, "The Last Bastion of Patriarchy," *Los Angeles Times*, 6 November 1994, Section M, pg. 5.

38. "1 in 4 Work in Women-Owned Firms In US," *Los Angeles Times*, 27 March 1997, Section D, pg. 2.

39. Braze, David, "Wake-up Call for Women," www.fool.com, 13 November 2000.

40 Brock, Fred, "Taking Hold of the Purse Strings, and Holding Their Own," *New York Times*, 20 October 1996, National edition, pg. 8.

41. Schembari, James, "New College Sticker Shock: Junior's Credit Card Bill," *New York Times*, 27 February 2000, National edition, Business section, pg. 12.

Bibliography

Agnes, Michael, ed. *Webster's New World Pocket Dictionary, Third Edition*. New York: MacMillan, 1997, pg. 158.

Alcott, Louisa May. *Little Women.* Boston, 1868.

Austen, Jane. *Pride and Prejudice.* London, 1813.

Austen, Jane. *Sense and Sensibility.* London, 1811.

Beardstown Ladies Investment Club with Leslie Whitaker. *The Beardstown Ladies' Common-sense Investment Guide.* New York: Hyperion, 1994.

Broussard, Cheryl. *The Black Woman's Guide to Financial Independence.* Oakland, CA: Hyde Park Publishing, 1991.

Campbell, Bebe Moore. *What You Owe Me.* New York: G.P. Putnam's Sons, 2001.

Delany, Sarah Louise, et al. *Having Our Say: The Delany Sisters' First 100 Years.* New York: Kodansha International, 1993.

Dickens, Charles. *David Copperfield.* London, 1849.

Eliot, George. *Middlemarch: A Study of Provincial Life.* London, 1871.

Hailey, Elizabeth Forsythe. *A Woman of Independent Means.* New York: Viking Press, 1978.

Oxford English Dictionary U.S Edition. Oxford: Oxford University Press, 1985.

SARK. *Eat Mangoes Naked: Finding Pleasure Everywhere and Dancing with the Pits.* New York: Fireside Books, 2001.

See, Carolyn. *Dreaming: Hard Luck and Good Times in America.* New York: Random House, 1995.

See, Carolyn. *The Handyman.* New York: Random House, 1999.

Stowers, James E. *Yes You Can – Achieve Financial Independence.* Kansas City, MO: Deer Publications, 1992.